Box.

Gunpowder Plots

Gunpowder Plots

BRENDA BUCHANAN
DAVID CANNADINE
JUSTIN CHAMPION
DAVID CRESSY
PAULINE CROFT
ANTONIA FRASER
MIKE JAY

ALLEN LANE
an imprint of
PENGUIN BOOKS

ALLEN LANE

Published by the Penguin Group
Penguin Books Ltd, 80 Strand, London WC2R ORL, England
Penguin Group (USA) Inc., 375 Hudson Street, New York, New York 10014, USA
Penguin Group (Canada), 90 Eglinton Avenue East, Suite 700, Toronto,
Ontario, Canada M4P 3YZ (a division of Pearson Penguin Canada Inc.)
Penguin Ireland, 25 St Stephen's Green, Dublin 2, Ireland (a division of Penguin Books Ltd)
Penguin Group (Australia), 250 Camberwell Road, Camberwell, Victoria 3124, Australia
(a division of Pearson Australia Group Pty Ltd)
Penguin Books India Pvt Ltd, 11 Community Centre, Panchsheel Park,
New Delhi – 110 017, India
Penguin Group (NZ), cnr Airborne and Rosedale Roads, Albany,
Auckland 1310, New Zealand (a division of Pearson New Zealand Ltd)
Penguin Books (South Africa) (Pty) Ltd, 24 Sturdee Avenue,
Rosebank 2196, South Africa

Penguin Books Ltd, Registered Offices: 80 Strand, London WC2R ORL, England

www.penguin.com

First published 2005
1

'The Fifth of November Remembered and Forgotten' copyright © David Cannadine, 2005;
'The Gunpowder Plot Fails' copyright © Pauline Croft, 2005; 'The Gunpowder Plot Succeeds'
copyright © Antonia Fraser, 2004, first published in *What Might Have Been*, edited by
Andrew Roberts; 'Four Hundred Years of Festivities' copyright © David Cressy, 1992,
first published in *Myths of the English*, edited by Roy Porter; 'Popes and Guys and
Anti-Catholicism' copyright © Justin Champion, 2005; 'Bonfire Night in Lewes'
copyright © Mike Jay, 2005; 'Making Fireworks' copyright © Brenda Buchanan, 2005

The moral right of the authors has been asserted

Set in 10/13.75 pt Linotype Sabon
Typeset by Rowland Phototypesetting Ltd, Bury St Edmunds, Suffolk
Printed in Great Britain by Clays Ltd, St Ives plc

A CIP catalogue record for this book is available from the British Library

ISBN 0-713-99886-5

Contents

List of Illustrations

The Fifth of November Remembered and Forgotten

DAVID CANNADINE

> Please to remember the Fifth of November,
> Gunpowder Treason and Plot.
> We know no reason why Gunpowder Treason
> Should ever be forgot.

At first sight, it seems strange that across four hundred years our nation has been annually commemorating an event that did *not* happen: namely, the failed attempt by Guy Fawkes and his fellow Catholic conspirators to blow up the Houses of Parliament in London at the beginning of a new legislative session on 5 November 1605. They were arrested, they were tortured, they were tried and they were executed. As such, they shared the fate of many conspirators who are labelled freedom fighters by their supporters, or derided as rebels and anarchists by their opponents, and who get caught by the very authorities they seek to overthrow. They lose, they suffer, they die, and their story ends, while the regime endures that they vainly sought to change. To be sure, the stakes were very high in November 1605: if the gunpowder had exploded, the entire Commons and Lords, plus King James I and his court, would have been blown to oblivion, in a destructive carnage that might have surpassed that of 9/11 in terms of numbers killed, and would certainly have exceeded it in terms of the collective might and power of those who had been taken out. Put in the Bush-and-Blair language of our own day, the foiling of the Gunpowder Plot was thus an outstandingly successful pre-emptive strike against what would now be described as the forces of organized, fanatical, religiously motivated terrorism.

But is this sufficient to explain why (and how) Guy Fawkes and his co-conspirators have enjoyed four centuries of demonized immortality, rather than of ignominious oblivion? It seems unlikely, for during that period, England's ritual calendar of commemorative events has been constantly evolving and transformed, and many once-secure festivals, commemorating what seemed to be important (indeed, iconic) national events, have subsequently fallen away: among them Armada Day, Oak Apple Day, Waterloo Day, Primrose Day, Empire Day, and so on. To be sure, Remembrance Day was successfully invented after the First World War, and it is still going strong; but it is not yet a hundred years old, and it may not survive the passing of the present queen's reign. Thus regarded, the Fifth of November is the only major date, not directly derived from the lifecycle of Jesus Christ, which has endured in our popular national calendar for so long. It is, then, an occasion easily taken for granted, but also in need of historical explanation and analysis. The essays gathered here attempt to do just that, and in so doing, they demonstrate how it has survived and evolved across the centuries, and what has been remembered (and forgotten) during the course of that survival and evolution; and they also make plain what a many-sided and multifaceted occasion it has almost always been.

As Pauline Croft explains, the genesis of the Gunpowder Plot must be sought in the complex mixture of hopes and anxieties with which English Catholics greeted the accession of James I on the death of Queen Elizabeth in March 1603. Initially, it seemed as though the new king would treat his

Catholic subjects with more kindly tolerance than his predecessor, but within little more than a year these anticipations
had been disappointed. To a small group of committed Catholic
conspirators, of whom Guy Fawkes was one, the only way
forward now seemed to be to assassinate the king, and to
proclaim his daughter Princess Elizabeth as (they hoped) a more
malleable and pro-Catholic queen. What would have happened had they succeeded? Antonia Fraser's imaginative essay
in counter-factual history seeks to answer just that question,
opening as it does with the coronation of Queen Elizabeth II (as
the nominally Catholic Princess Elizabeth had now become) on
15 January 1606. Meanwhile, her surviving brother, Charles,
who was nominally Protestant, had fled to Scotland, where
he had been proclaimed king. Eventually, Catholic England and
Protestant Scotland might well have gone to war, Charles might
still have lost his head, a Catholic, pro-French monarchy would
have been established in England, and the Fifth of November
would have been celebrated as a very different sort of occasion
from that with which later generations have been familiar.

But the plot failed, and as David Cressy points out, the
Fifth of November subsequently became the most enduring
anniversary in the nation's Protestant calendar, taking on
different meanings, and attracting the support of different
groups, at different times, and for different purposes. During
the seventeenth century, it was a Protestant celebration of providential deliverance, often enjoying both elite and popular
involvement. Under the Hanoverians, elite observance was more
dutiful than enthusiastic, while among the lower orders it
became an occasion for riot, disturbance and displays of misrule
which lasted well into the nineteenth century. Only at the
end of Queen Victoria's reign, and on into the early twentieth
century, did bonfires and fireworks become more respectable,
with more children participating, and with shouts of 'penny for

3

the Guy'. But despite these changes, there was, throughout, an underlying theme of militant, national Protestantism, which was always the key to its survival. Put the other way, as Justin Champion reminds us, this meant that the Fifth of November has always been an explicitly or latently anti-Catholic event: indeed, for well over the first hundred years of its existence, it was the Pope who was burned in effigy, and it was only in the late eighteenth century that Guy Fawkes became the central figure who was now consigned to the flames.

These national changes and developments are vividly illuminated in Mike Jay's essay, which explores Bonfire Night in Lewes, a generally quaint and quiet market town in East Sussex, where the observances retain much of the riotous and oppositional character by which they have been characterized since the late eighteenth century. For reasons that are not wholly clear, the town remains to this day a 'strong citadel of Bonfiredom', and for this one night only it combines civic pride and civic disobedience in a particularly resonant combination: in addition to Guy Fawkes, other figures recently burned in effigy have included Bill Clinton, George W. Bush, John Major and Gordon Brown. But the Fifth of November needs to be understood not only in local but also in global terms, and this is the purpose of Brenda Buchanan's concluding contribution. Fireworks and Bonfire Night are inextricably linked in the popular mind; but as she explains, this was not a pre-ordained union. Getting gunpowder from China to England was a complex and protracted business; and thereafter fireworks were more broadly associated with military triumphs, royal occasions and civic ceremonial. Only in the late nineteenth century did they become the indispensable accompaniment to the Fifth of November itself.

All of which is simply to say that the history of Bonfire Night is a long, complex, changing and contested one, which has rarely received the attention that it merits, and which may be approached in a variety of (not always compatible) ways. From one perspective, that history may be regarded as a consensual display of shared national values, collective identity and religious moderation; from another, it can be seen as a sustained display of establishment exclusiveness, national xenophobia and religious bigotry; from yet a third it can be looked at as a sign of vigorous popular protest, committed radical politics and technological cosmopolitanism. There are thus many narratives of the Fifth of November, and they do not all lead to the same conclusions. That, in turn, may help to explain its unique longevity: it has meant many things to many people in many places at many times. Nor is that history over yet. In recent years the growing concern about terrorism and about health and safety, the decline in a shared sense of national and Protestant identity, and the alternative, American allure of Hallowe'en, have led some to fear that the Fifth of November is on the way out. But such anxieties have often been expressed across the four hundred years since 1605, and they have never yet been borne out.

Are things different in 2005? How will Guy Fawkes Night look in 2010? If the varied, disputed, unpredictable history of this event is any guide, then it is impossible to predict how it will evolve in the future. As the bonfires burn, the fireworks fizzle and the sparklers sparkle in this anniversary year, they may seem the dying embers of an outmoded festival that no longer resonates in the secular, multicultural, globalized world we now inhabit, where the old national identities, built around (among other things) royalty and religion, have lost some of the significance they once had. But it may be, in an era when many Britons are hostile to 'Europe', with (as they see it) its historic and alien connotations of Catholicism and authoritarianism, and when others are no less opposed to what they regard (and

7

regret) as the Americanization of our culture, of which the recent rise of Hallowe'en is but one more disturbing sign, that the Fifth of November will take on a new identity as a focus for protest against our nation's precarious position, increasingly threatened by two powerful (and predatory?) continents. 'Guy Fawkes for UKIP' may not seem a wholly plausible slogan. But stranger things have happened during this re-remarkably long-lived festival of fun and fire, playfulness and patriotism, inclusion and exclusion. Only time will tell.

CHAPTER ONE

The Gunpowder Plot Fails

PAULINE CROFT

On 9 November 1605, four days after the discovery of the Gunpowder Plot only hours before the state opening of Parliament, the shaken members of the House of Lords and the House of Commons were sent home. The government of James I wanted to concentrate on pursuing the terrorists and bringing them to justice, without the additional distractions of managing a parliamentary session. On 21 January 1606, after a lengthy Christmas break, the Lords and Commons reconvened. The prolonged holiday had done little to lessen the general sense of shock. Both Houses were still stunned by the near-miss of the planned atrocity which would have killed and maimed so many of their members. As the Attorney General, the great lawyer Sir Edward Coke, commented sombrely: 'No Man can aggravate [exaggerate] the Powder Treason. To tell it, and know it, is enough.' Coke's words point to the immediate impact of the plot and help to explain its enduring place in British historical consciousness. However, 'to tell it, and know it' we must begin much earlier.

By 1590 Queen Elizabeth, born in 1533, had lived longer than either her father or her grandfather, and her subjects were ever more aware that her days were numbered. North of the Border, James VI of Scotland was manoeuvring energetically to maximize his chances of succeeding to her throne. James was the queen's nearest blood relative, like her a direct descendant of the first Tudor monarch, Henry VII. After his birth in June 1566 his mother Mary Queen of Scots had publicly hoped that he would be the first ruler to unite the kingdoms of England and Scotland. Elizabeth granted a pension to the impecunious Scottish king in 1586 and promised that she would not undercut any right or title that he possessed. Further than that she would not go. As the years passed James became increasingly agitated that he had never been officially proclaimed her heir.

To ensure his accession, the king planned both to build up English support and to disarm any foreign opposition. He corresponded with the young earl of Essex, Elizabeth's last favourite, hoping that Essex's inside information on court politics would ease his way to the throne. Many of the earl's followers were Catholics, members of the post-Reformation religious minority in England that bore the burden of the recusancy laws (aimed at those who would not attend their Protestant parish churches). The laws were unevenly enforced, and many low-profile Catholics got off virtually scot-free, but the psychological burden was considerable and most Catholic males knew their career prospects were blighted if they adhered openly to the old religion. Within the small Catholic community was a much smaller group of proudly committed, faithful *dévots* to whom the recusancy laws might bring grave financial hardship and years in prison. For Catholic priests, particularly those belonging to the new Counter-Reformation order of the Jesuits, service in England meant disguise, the constant fear of betrayal and possibly a hideous death by hanging, drawing and quartering.

Essex occasionally indulged in a rhetoric of tolerance towards those Catholics who were politically loyal. As a result, many of them followed him in offering their service to the Scottish claimant to the English throne. In Europe, the Protestant regimes of the Dutch and the Scandinavian monarchies would not oppose James, but Spain, the leading power of Catholic Europe, might make trouble. In 1588, as the Armada sailed, Philip II had announced that his daughter, the Infanta Isabella, descended from the English King Edward III, would replace Elizabeth as queen. The Armada was defeated, but Isabella's claim remained a part of official Spanish policy, although she had few if any Catholic supporters in England. In 1595 the Scottish Catholic gentleman John Ogilvy of Poury began a journey across Europe which included a visit to Spain, where he indicated that James might become a Spanish ally and possibly also a Catholic. This informal probe was followed after the death of Philip II in 1598 by the mission of another Catholic, Lord Robert Sempill, who hoped to persuade the new king, Philip III, to recognize James as Elizabeth's heir. Neither of these diplomatic missions was successful but they convinced the Scottish Jesuits resident in Madrid that their king was a friend to Catholics.

The attitude of the papacy might be crucial in swinging the support of other Catholic states such as Savoy and Tuscany. Here, James turned to his advantage the conversion to Catholicism of his wife, Anne of Denmark, who had been a Lutheran on her arrival in Scotland in 1590. Anne came under attack from the Scottish Presbyterian Kirk, which deplored her extravagance and love of court entertainments. The Kirk's censorious hostility alienated the young queen from its dour Protestantism. Her close friend Henriette, the French-born wife of James's supporter the marquis of Huntly, was influential in leading the queen to take instruction in Catholicism. In 1599 James wrote to Pope Clement VIII on a minor ecclesiastical matter, signing himself in Latin as 'your most obedient son'. Then Queen Anne wrote to the Pope and to Cardinal Borghese, announcing her conversion. Her ambiguous use of the royal 'we' gave rise to hopes in Rome that the king would soon convert, and in 1602 Clement VIII urged James to do so. The king's other

Continental overtures were rather less successful. Ferdinand I, the wealthy grand duke of Tuscany, conducted a courteous correspondence but sidelined James's suggestion that a Tuscan bride would be very acceptable for the king's eldest son, Prince Henry. Once again, however, the news spread that James was a friend of Catholics, and neither the papacy nor Tuscany showed any interest in opposing his claim to succeed the English queen. The Infanta Isabella, by 1599 married to her cousin the Archduke Albert and resident in Brussels, was also hopeful of the king's conversion. 'The Archdukes', as the royal couple were known, were keener than Philip III to end the stale Anglo-Spanish war that had begun nearly fifteen years earlier, and proved disastrous for the Netherlands' commerce and prosperity. Isabella was averse to any Spanish attempt to prevent James's ultimate accession to Elizabeth's throne.

So the king's strategy of making overtures to foreign powers was effective in deflecting any Catholic-led opposition to his claim. Much more important, however, was the quiet revolution that took place in Anglo-Scottish affairs in 1601. Sir Robert Cecil, who had succeeded his father Lord Burghley as Elizabeth's chief adviser, was aware from dispatches sent from Scotland that the king was dangerously restive over the unresolved succession. Then in February the earl of Essex, in disgrace after his failure to put down a major revolt in Ireland, led a band of young malcontents into the streets of London in a rash attempt to evict his enemies from court. The chaotic rising failed. Essex was quickly tried and sent to the block, leaving James without a confidant at the English court. Cecil was deeply perturbed by the revolt, which suggested that England might become ungovernable in the queen's declining years. In the spring, when Scottish envoys arrived in Whitehall, Cecil made it clear that, when the time came, he would support the Scottish claim. A discreet agreement was reached that he would write privately to the king, joining in a secret correspondence with James already being conducted by a group of pro-Scottish Englishmen, most notably the crypto-Catholic nobleman Lord Henry Howard. The rapprochement was a crucial turning point. After spring 1601 James, by far the strongest candidate for Elizabeth's throne, was acting in concert with Cecil, the leading member of the English Privy Council. It would be virtually impossible to derail his accession. Reassured, the king stopped sabre-rattling and promised that he would follow Cecil's advice, biding his time patiently until Elizabeth died.

The correspondence between James and Cecil inevitably touched on religion. In his book *Basilicon Doron*, the king made it plain that he regretted that the Presbyterian Reformation in Scotland had lacked 'the prince's order', a compliment to the contrasting English experience of a royal Supreme Governor over the Church. To Cecil, James expounded his views on Catholics. 'I will never allow in my conscience that the blood of any man shall be shed for diversity of opinions in religion,' he wrote, 'but I would be sorry that Catholics should so multiply as they might be able to practise their old principles on us.' Unlike many Protestants, James accepted that the Roman Catholic Church was 'our mother church', but he also viewed it as corrupt, and he did not wish Catholic numbers to increase. Cecil admitted that he loathed seeing Catholic priests die by hanging, drawing and quartering, but his tolerance did not go quite so far as the king's. To the earl of Northumberland, who wrote on behalf of the English Catholics (although denying he was one himself), James set out his future policies clearly. 'As for the Catholics, I will neither persecute any that will be quiet and give but an outward obedience to the law, neither will I spare to advance any of them that will by good service worthily deserve it.' This suggested that once he was in England, James would follow Elizabeth in requiring outward conformity, but would also follow the course he adopted in Scotland, where he angered the Kirk by his warm acceptance of Catholic nobles such as the Huntlys.

These carefully qualified royal remarks were often interpreted much more generously. Northumberland's kinsman Thomas Percy, who often acted as a messenger for the earl, visited James at Holyrood palace in 1602 and was convinced that he would offer a general Catholic toleration on his accession. Percy spread the good news, and when Elizabeth finally died on 24 March 1603, English Catholics openly rejoiced. Some, like Sir Thomas Tresham in Northamptonshire and Lord Arundell of Wardour in Dorset, overrode local officials in their eagerness to proclaim the king ahead of official instructions. Others like the priest George Blackwell contributed barrels of wine to celebratory bonfire parties. Fr. Henry Garnet, Superior of the English Jesuits, wrote enthusiastically in April that 'A golden time we have of unexpected freedom ... Great hope is of toleration; and so general a consent of Catholics in the king's proclaiming, it seemeth God will work much.' Exiled priests and lay people began to flock back across the Channel. It was even suggested that the English Catholics would soon have a formal legal toleration comparable to that established for the French Huguenots in 1598 by the Edict of Nantes.

In April 1603 the king left Edinburgh for London. From Newcastle, he wrote to the Privy Council explaining that many came to him with grievances, and suggesting that a public acknowledgement might be made of 'severities' in the late queen's time – clearly a gesture to Catholics. As he visited York he was petitioned for toleration by both a Benedictine priest in disguise and a Catholic layman. In June, as Queen Anne followed her husband south, a group of Catholic ladies gathered at York to urge her to use her influence towards a toleration. In

July, just before his coronation, James received Tresham and other leading Catholic gentry at Hampton Court. They brought a petition urging a public debate on the position of Catholics, aiming to show that a toleration offered no threat to stability. Instead, the king told them that he would suspend the monthly recusancy fines so long as the Catholic community continued to support both king and state. Records of the fines show that they fell rapidly, proving that James kept his word.

So far everything had gone fairly well for the Catholics. Then in June and July came the revelation of the Bye and Main Plots. The Bye Plot, so called because it was the lesser in import-ance, was a mad attempt led by a priest named William Watson to hold the king to ransom until he declared a toleration. The Main Plot was more drastic, and more secular. Led by Lord Cobham and other notables including Sir Walter Ralegh, it aimed to get rid of the Scottish king and his 'cubs', instead placing his English-born cousin Lady Arbella Stuart on the throne. It was the first sign of English disenchantment with the new Scottish regime. Neither plot came anywhere near success, not least because two Catholic priests got wind of the Bye Plot and tipped off the Privy Council. English Catholics reacted with horror at the folly of the plotters, and James accepted that the community as a whole was not tarred by the disloyalty of Watson and the rest. Even so, it was the first sign that the king's dealings with Catholics might rebound against him.

By winter 1604 James was securely settled in England and his earlier conciliatory stance was hardening. In January at Hampton Court he conferred with the other end of the religious spectrum, the Puritans, who petitioned for further reformation in the Protestant Church of England. They got little by way of concessions, with the king asserting his support for bishops and showing his distaste for what he saw as nitpicking on un-important issues. Early in February he made a speech in which he mentioned the Bye Plot and sounded much less open towards Catholic petitioning. He assured the Privy Council of his utter detestation of 'their superstitious religion'. On 22 February a proclamation was issued, attacking the papacy's claim to dispense with the king's subjects' natural obedience to him and ordering Catholic priests to leave the realm by 19 March 1604. James much preferred exile to execution. In the first Parliament of the reign, summoned for 19 March 1604, a new recusancy bill was promoted, confirming all the Elizabethan legislative penalties on Catholics. It received the royal assent in July 1604, and in the same month, at Warwick, two priests who had refused to leave the country were executed in the usual barbaric fashion, the first victims of the reign. By late 1604 the recusancy fines were once again being collected.

Even during the early months of 1603, while the king had been reaching out towards Catholics, some expressed their disappointment. Many Catholics growing to manhood in the 1590s were less quiescent than their parents and hoped that James's accession would signal not just an easing of conditions, but genuine 'regime change'. They were prepared to use physical violence in pursuit of it. Robert Catesby, the tall, handsome and charismatic son of a wealthy Catholic family from Warwickshire, was a follower of Essex and fought in his doomed rebellion of 1601. Alongside Catesby fought Francis Tresham, his cousin and close friend, son of the Northamptonshire landowner Sir Thomas Tresham. Jack and Kit Wright, both noted swordsmen and brothers-in-law of Thomas Percy, also fought in the rebellion. They were at school at St Peter's, York, with Guy Fawkes, who left England in 1592 to fight in the armies of Catholic Spain in the Netherlands against the rebel Dutch. Catesby was related to Robert and Thomas Wintour of Worcestershire. Like Fawkes, Thomas was a former soldier in the Netherlands, and his uncle was a priest who had been hanged, drawn and quartered. The Wintour home, Huddington Court, was known as a priests' refuge, and in late autumn 1601 Tom Wintour journeyed to Spain on behalf of Catesby, Tresham and others left leaderless after the downfall of Essex. He offered support in case of a future Spanish invasion of England to aid Catholics, but got little more than promises of financial assistance. When the queen died, the Spanish had formulated only an impractical policy that vaguely inclined to support a (non-existent) English Catholic contender for her throne.

Wintour was not the only member of the group that originally looked to Spain. Guy Fawkes also travelled to Spain and in July 1603 wrote a memorandum, still in the Spanish archives, which scorned James and insisted that he was 'a heretic ... [hoping] in a short time to have all of the papist sect driven out of England'. Fawkes revealed his fiercely anti-Scottish streak, emphasizing the dislike of the English nobility for the Scottish newcomers and arguing that the natural hostility between them would make it impossible to reconcile the two nations for long. He warned the Spanish court that any peace overtures from James should be treated as subterfuges and ignored. Fawkes was too late, for in spring 1603, 'the Archdukes'-had immediately sent an envoy to the new king to congratulate him. Spain grudgingly followed their lead. Philip III, using the opportunity of the new reign to end the state of hostility that had endured between England and Spain since the Armada, thought that his envoy Juan de Tassis should insist on toleration for Catholics as part of the negotiations. But on arrival in England Tassis realized this would be impossible and advised that the matter should be set aside until after the peace treaty was finalized.

Catesby and his friends had already begun to lose faith in Spain. In winter 1604 Tom Wintour was summoned to London and found Catesby and Jack Wright at Catesby's house in Lambeth, across the Thames from Westminster. Catesby announced that he had thought of a way 'at one instant' to deliver English Catholics from their bonds, without foreign help. 'In a word, it was to blow up the Parliament house with gunpowder; for said he, in that place have they done us all the mischief [by the recusancy laws] and perchance God hath designed that place for their punishment.' Catesby probably got the idea on reading the proclamation that came out on 18 January, announcing that the new king would shortly call a Parliament. Wintour was taken aback, because a failure would be catastrophic, but Catesby insisted 'that the nature of the disease' required 'so sharp a remedy'. His mesmeric self-confidence won over the initially reluctant Wintour: 'I told him Yes, in this or what else soever, if he resolved upon it, I would venture my life.' However, as a last-ditch effort, they decided to contact the Constable of Castile, the chief Spanish envoy for the forthcoming peace treaty recently arrived in Flanders, to see if he would help the English Catholics in his negotiations. They received a sympathetic response but no promises, and the Catholic exiles at Brussels were convinced that everyone was so desperate for peace with England that nothing would be allowed to stand in its way. In April, Guy Fawkes was waiting at Dunkirk to cross into England, and encountered Tom Wintour who told him that they 'were upon a resolution to do somewhat in England if the peace with Spain helped us not'. Shortly afterwards, Thomas Percy came to London, and burst out at the gathering, 'Shall we always, gentlemen, talk and never do anything?' Their resolve was stiffened, and in May the inner group of five men met at a lodging behind St Clements in the Strand. They took an oath of secrecy, then heard Mass in another room and took the sacrament, whereupon Catesby disclosed to Fawkes and Thomas Percy his plan, already familiar to Wright and Wintour. The priest who celebrated the Mass, Fr. John Gerard SJ, was not present at their discussions.

By this time the first session of Parliament had opened on 19 March 1604 and was likely to close before the summer set in with its usual threat of plague. On 24 May Thomas Percy used his links with his kinsman Northumberland to lease a small house adjacent to the House of Lords' chamber in the old palace of Westminster. The idea was to drive a shaft – 'the mine' – from the cellars through to the foundations of the chamber. Then gunpowder could be ferried across the Thames at night from Lambeth and hidden there. A sixth man, Robert Keyes, was brought in as keeper of Catesby's house and its gunpowder store. Before much could be done, Parliament was prorogued on 7 July with its next meeting announced for 7 February 1605.

The treaty negotiations between Spain, England and Spanish Flanders were concluded in August 1604. Scotland had never been at war with Spain so James signed solely in his capacity as king of England. There was no mention of toleration for the English Catholics in the treaty. A scheme for buying out the recusancy fines with Spanish money was mooted, but nothing came of it, although Spain was happy to promise lavish, no-strings-attached pensions to the leading English Councillors. When the Constable sailed from Dover on 30 August 1604, it was painfully obvious to English Catholics that nothing had been achieved that would make their lot any easier. More bad news followed, as James commissioned Lord Chancellor Ellesmere to preside over a Privy Council committee to 'exterminate' Jesuits, other priests and lay Catholics who were aiming to subvert the king's subjects from their lawful allegiance.

The plotters must have been relieved to leave Westminster behind for a healthier summer in the country, but there is no indication that they took trouble to ascertain the exact terms of the treaty before continuing with their plan. They had already abandoned any hopes of Spain. They agreed to meet again at the start of the Michaelmas law term, which would give them time to dig the mine before the new parliamentary session intended for February 1605. Unfortunately, their conveniently placed house was then requisitioned by the commissioners for the king's proposed but eventually unsuccessful constitutional Union between England and Scotland, who were summoned to meet at Westminister on 20 October 1604. It was not until a fortnight before Christmas 1604 that the plotters were once again in possession and could start to dig, only to learn on 28 December that lingering plague outbreaks had forced a further prorogation of Parliament until 3 October 1605. They suspended work until early February 1605, when they rowed all the gunpowder over from Lambeth and concealed it in the house. The time spent digging and propping up the mine was passed in discussing how they could get hold of the young Prince Charles and his sister Elizabeth. The heir, Prince Henry, would attend the Parliament with his father, and 'happily' meet the same fate. For the coup to be successful, it would be necessary to have all the surviving royals in their hands. Through the patronage of his kinsman Northumberland, in June 1604 Percy was made a gentleman pensioner (one of the king's bodyguard), and promised to use his position at court to capture Charles. The four-year-old boy only arrived from Scotland in October 1604 and was regarded as sickly: no one took him too seriously, since he might not survive. Moreover, the plotters were working on the usual gender assumptions of their sex and class, so Princess Elizabeth seemed likely to make a more malleable puppet monarch, and she figured more largely in their plans than her younger brother.

March 1605 marked the beginning of a new phase of the plot, when Robert Wintour (Tom's brother), Kit Wright (Jack's brother) and John Grant (the Wintours' brother-in-law) were let into the secret. Then, just at the point when their tunnel encountered the redoubtable stone foundations of the Lords' chamber, a new opportunity arose. The street-level chamber or vault between the tunnel and the Lords' first-floor meeting place was used for coal storage, and unexpectedly became available for rent. A lease was secured on 25 March for £4 per year. The chamber formed part of the warren of medieval kitchen buildings of the original palace of Westminster, abandoned as a royal family residence after a disastrous fire in 1512. It made the task far easier since they could stack the gunpowder directly under the House of Lords. Once again, they broke off for the summer and Fawkes went back to Flanders. Catesby, the paymaster for the whole venture, surveyed his finances on a visit to Bath, where he met Percy. It was agreed he could recruit some others to help bear the costs. So Ambrose Rookwood, Sir Everard Digby and Francis Tresham joined the inner circle, although Tresham was so agitated on hearing what was planned that he tried to bribe Catesby to abandon the plot. On 3 October 1605 Parliament was prorogued again until 5 November. In the entourage of Lord Monteagle, Tom Wintour attended the prorogation ceremony in the Lords, where he must have reflected that, if the gunpowder secretly stored below went off, he would die in the company of a large number of noblemen and Privy Councillors.

By late October the plotters were congregating in London. Wintour and Fawkes brought in some fresh gunpowder in case the original stores were damp, and everything seemed to be in place. However, on 26 October 1605, just as four of the leading lords of the Privy Council – the earls of Salisbury, Suffolk, Northampton and Worcester – were sitting down for a convivial supper at Whitehall, a letter was brought in to them by Lord Monteagle. An erstwhile Catholic and a follower of Essex,

Monteagle had been helped out of trouble in 1601 by Robert Cecil (created Viscount Cranborne for his services in crafting the peace with Spain, then earl of Salisbury in May 1605). Monteagle publicly emphasized his new-found Protestantism, but was intimately linked to Catholic circles by his marriage to a sister of Francis Tresham and by his sister Mary's marriage to the Worcestershire recusant Thomas Habington of Hindlip. Even worse, Tom Wintour, at the heart of the plot, acted as Monteagle's secretary. In summer 1605 Lord Salisbury was already receiving disturbing rumours of a Catholic conspiracy in the making. Much comment was aroused by a very public pilgrimage in August 1605 to Holywell, the old shrine of St Winifrid in north Wales, led by Fr. Henry Garnet, Superior of the English Jesuits. But as yet Salisbury had few specific pieces of information. The letter brought by Monteagle (and most probably covertly written by him, using information he had gathered from his Catholic contacts) included a warning to stay away – 'devise some excuse to shift of your attendance at this Parliament' – since 'a terrible blow' would be struck. Salisbury probably suspected the worst at that point, but it was agreed that no immediate measures should be taken until the king returned from his hunting. However, Salisbury's intelligencer George Southwick redoubled his efforts, diligently riding around for further information.

On Friday 1 November, Salisbury placed the Monteagle letter before the king in his gallery at Whitehall. James thought of his father Lord Darnley's murder in the deliberate explosion at Kirk o' Field in Edinburgh in 1567, and wondered if, once again, gunpowder was involved. On Saturday the Privy Council decided that Lord Chamberlain Suffolk, in charge of preparing the old palace of Westminster for the Parliament, should search both above and below the chambers used for the meeting places. Meanwhile, on Sunday 27 October Catesby learned of the Monteagle letter and feared their plot was betrayed. He sent Fawkes to check their rented chamber, but was reassured when he reported that nothing had been touched. Both Catesby and Tom Wintour suspected Francis Tresham of betraying them, but his vehement oaths managed to convince them of his innocence. Reinforced by Thomas Percy, who agreed that they should see their plan through, Catesby refused to back down. On 4 November Percy rode to Syon House on the Thames to see his kinsman Northumberland, fishing for anything suspicious that might indicate the earl had heard something of the plot. Percy sensed he knew nothing and did not warn Northumberland to stay away from the state opening. Later on the same day, Fawkes went to the vault with a slow match and a watch given him by Percy to check the time. Astonishingly, Lord Chamberlain Suffolk, making his rounds of the palace accompanied by Lord Monteagle among others, went into the chamber and encountered Fawkes, whom he took to be some sort of servant. Suffolk noted the large pile of brushwood and faggots (concealing the gunpowder) but was satisfied when told it belonged to the tenant of the house, Mr Thomas Percy of the gentleman pensioners. The noblemen proceeded on their tour of inspection.

On their return to court, Monteagle expressed some surprise that Thomas Percy should be renting a vault in Westminster when he had his own house in London. He also commented that Percy was a Catholic, surmising that Percy might well be the author of the anonymous warning letter, since he and Monteagle had been friends. The king then ordered a further search of the cellars and undercrofts of the old palace, this time undertaken by Sir Thomas Knyvet, a Westminster Justice of the Peace and a member of the king's privy chamber. Knyvet was also an old friend of Salisbury, with whom he had sat for the borough of Westminster in the 1584 Parliament, the

ARREST OF GUY FAWKES.

young Cecil's first session. In order not to raise any alert, it was given out that they were looking for hangings that had been embezzled from the stores. About midnight on 4 November they reached Fawkes in the vault, booted and fully clothed. Knyvet had him arrested, and his men found the gunpowder, packed in thirty-six barrels, under the woodpile. Fawkes gave his name as John Johnson, a servant of Thomas Percy.

The plotters intended that on the morning of Tuesday 5 November Fawkes would light the length of slow match as soon as the king came into the Lords (presumably by hearing the noise overhead) and get away across the Thames before the explosion. Meanwhile Sir Everard Digby and his servants established themselves at the Red Lion in Dunchurch, under the guise of a hunting party. As soon as he learned of the plot's success, Catesby would leave London for the Midlands where he would meet with Digby to mastermind the Catholic rising that formed the next stage of the plot. They would seize Princess Elizabeth from Coombe Abbey near Rugby, the home of her governor, Lord Harington, and proclaim her queen. But little of this had been fully worked out: as the Jesuit Fr. Oswald Tesimond later commented, 'They left all at random.' Once the news of Fawkes's arrest was out, Catesby, Percy and John Wright fled north, meeting the assembled Catholic gentry at Dunchurch that evening. One of the servants at the Red Lion later recalled hearing a man speak out of a casement window: 'I doubt wee are all betrayde.' The majority of the huntsmen melted away, refusing to involve themselves in the conspiracy.

The ringleaders were not ready to give in. Late at night on 5 November they raided the stables of Warwick Castle for fresh horses, then spent two days moving from one Catholic 'safe house' to another, including Huddington Grange, the

Wintour home, where they received communion. No new supporters joined them and the recusant Thomas Habington of Hindlip, married to Monteagle's sister, refused them shelter. On 7 November they reached Holbeach House in Staffordshire, home of one of the Dunchurch hunting party. Utterly exhausted by strain, fear and their hours of riding, the plotters carelessly spread out before the fire some damp gunpowder taken from one of the houses in which they had rested. It exploded, burning Catesby and Rookwood and blinding John Grant. They already knew that they were being followed by government forces, and the terrible, coincidental explosion convinced them that they had lost their great gamble. Morale collapsed. Jack Wright suggested to Catesby that they should blow themselves up with the remaining gunpowder. Tom Wintour, who had been out of the house trying in vain to raise some Catholic help, asked on his return what they would do. Catesby, the Wright brothers, Thomas Percy and the rest replied unhesitatingly, 'We mean here to die.' Wintour answered that he would do the same.

The following morning the sheriff of Worcestershire and his posse of at least two hundred men arrived outside Holbeach. In the exchange of fire, Jack and Kit Wright were killed. Thomas Percy and Robert Catesby were brought down by one shot that passed through both of them. Catesby managed to crawl back into the house, where he found a picture of the Virgin Mary and died clutching it. From beginning to end, the plot was all his work. Courageous, affluent and ruthless, he had used his forceful personality to bring others in, and exercised a compelling hold over them. Although Catesby paid occasional lip-service to the idea that they should save as many as possible of the crypto-Catholic noblemen who would attend the fatal state opening, he despised the men who had offered so little leadership to their beleaguered co-religionists. To Catesby, the peerage consisted mostly of 'atheists fools and cowards', so he did not concern himself with their fate. He never showed the slightest remorse for what he had planned to do.

Tom Wintour had wanted to die at Holbeach, but he was captured, shot in his right arm and unable to defend himself. Also captured were the injured Ambrose Rookwood and the severely burned John Grant. These survivors were taken back to London, where others including Sir Everard Digby and Francis Tresham later joined them in the Tower. By 9 November Fawkes had been tortured and given six statements on the conspiracy, each fuller than the last. He reiterated that intense dislike of the Scots which had been evident on his visit to Spain. The king had at once proposed questions to be put to Fawkes, including a query about the authorship of a hostile libel that asserted that James would die for taking the unpopular title of 'King of Great Britain'. He immediately leaped to the conclusion that anti-Scots hatred was at the heart of the plot, and authorized 'the gentler tortures' first, with an escalation if necessary. However, Fawkes and Wintour were now the only survivors of the original plotters and their testimony would be vital. The shootout at Holbeach saved the government most of the task of hunting down survivors, as well as demonstrating beyond doubt that these were the guilty men. The Privy Council, initially so baffled by events that they sought help from the celebrity astrologer Simon Foreman, could feel by 9 November that they were back in control. The king's speech that day at the prorogation of Parliament was gracious, emphasizing that he believed the plot to be the work of a few fanatics rather than the whole Catholic community. He also exonerated Catholic monarchs abroad. He gave thanks that God had delivered them all from 'a roaring, nay a thundering sin of fire and brimstone'.

There was still unfinished business to attend to, and Northumberland was unable to rid himself of the shadow cast by his cousin Thomas Percy. The Privy Council suspected that

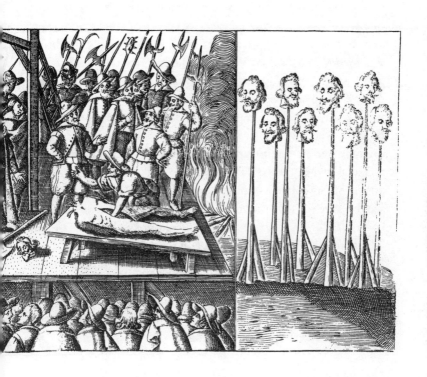

the plotters intended to use Northumberland as Protector, to guide Princess Elizabeth through her minority. As a result, the earl languished for years in the Tower, albeit in comfortable quarters. The surviving plotters – Fawkes, Tom and Robert Wintour, Everard Digby, John Grant, Robert Keyes, Ambrose Rookwood and Catesby's servant Thomas Bates – were tried on 27 January 1606, found guilty and executed over the next few days. The government was also keen to implicate the Catholic priests, and here the confession of Catesby's servant Thomas Bates proved invaluable. Before going to his own death, Bates incriminated Fr. John Gerard, who had said Mass at the initial meeting of May 1604, as well as Fr. Oswald Tesimond and above all Fr. Henry Garnet. In July 1605 Catesby had suffered a rare spasm of moral unease, and in confession revealed something of his plans to Tesimond. In great distress of mind Tesimond passed the information on to Garnet. Neither had revealed the plot to the authorities, although they tried to damp down any treasonable activity among Catholics whom they knew well. Gerard and Tesimond got away from England just in time, but Garnet was hunted down and tried on 28 March 1606. The elderly priest was hanged, drawn and quartered in May, but the spectacle seems to have dismayed those present. No one cried out the customary 'God save the king'.

On the evening of 5 November 1605, with Fawkes in custody and the plot foiled, there was a great outburst of bell-ringing. In addition, the inhabitants of London were encouraged to light bonfires to celebrate the providential deliverance of the king and his nobility. An Act was passed in 1606 for an annual public thanksgiving with appropriate sermons, and the day was kept as a religious occasion rather than a rambunctious social event. It was only in the later seventeenth century that effigies of the Pope were burned on the bonfires, and 'the guy', after Fawkes, appeared in the eighteenth century.

The long-lasting impact of the Gunpowder Plot must be put down in the first place to the grand scale of the intended atrocity. Unlike earlier Catholic plots against Queen Elizabeth herself, the Gunpowder Plot would have killed hundreds if not thousands, not only in the House of Lords but in the great fire which would surely have swept through the decrepit palace and out into the suburb of Westminster. Perhaps the second reason why the commemoration survived was simply that the story was so chillingly dramatic. More recently it has come to speak to our own ambiguous times. We are all too familiar with terrorism, and there is no doubt that, even though the word was not known in 1605, Protestant contemporaries (and many Catholics) regarded the plotters with all the horror reserved for murderous fanatics. Yet they were also tragic figures, remarkably brave and deeply religious men drawn into a doubtful cause. Led by the charismatic figure of Robert Catesby, they were driven by sustained state persecution to see themselves as heroes freeing their oppressed people. The final straw was the deliberately exploitative way in which King James first raised English Catholic hopes and then dashed them. To men like Robert Catesby, Thomas Percy, Guy Fawkes and Tom Wintour, by spring 1604 it was clear that they must either content themselves with idle talk, or take some action. The rest is history.

CHAPTER TWO

The Gunpowder Plot Succeeds

ANTONIA FRASER

The coronation of Queen Elizabeth II took place on a fine, fair day in January 1606 – the 15th to be precise, in honour of her glorious predecessor, the first Elizabeth, who had been crowned on that very day in 1559. This was not the only deliberate echo of that previous sacred festivity. Elizabeth I, who once said that 'In pompous ceremonies a secret of government doth much consist, for that the people are both naturally taken and help with exterior shows', would have understood the reasoning. At the same time she would have utterly abhorred the circumstances which had brought about this new coronation, less than three years after the accession to the throne of Elizabeth II's father, James I.

So the young Elizabeth Stuart, eldest daughter of King James and Queen Anne, had spent three nights before her coronation in the Tower as was customary for sovereigns, and as her father (and the great Elizabeth) had done in their time. She had then processed to Westminster Abbey through streets with fresh gravel flung down, where the windows were hung with banners. A canopy was carried over her head and an enormous mantle made from twenty-five yards of gold and silver tissue was wrapped around her. At the age of nine and a half, Elizabeth II might have been in danger of being dwarfed by her imposing surroundings. Fortunately she was tall for her age (taking after her late mother, or perhaps her grandmother, Mary Queen of

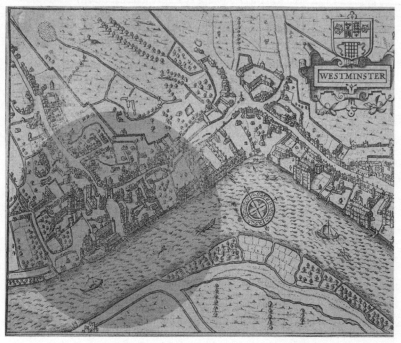

Shaded circle gives approximate blast area.

Scots), her appearance further enhanced by the dignity of her bearing, on which all commented. Elizabeth II was already showing signs of great beauty with her huge heavy-lidded hazel eyes and her delicate oval face; that was something which certainly excited the French ambassador. He was not used to a matrimonial prize such as this unmarried queen being, in his own words, so 'very well bred and handsome'.

The other aspect of the new queen's appearance noted by all the spectators both along the route and in the Abbey itself – but not mentioned publicly – was her extraordinary air of melancholy. It did not pass during the crowning itself, when it was as though the actual crown was weighing her head down; and it did not pass when the Lord Protector, Henry Percy, earl of Northumberland, escorted her back down the aisle of the Abbey. Yet her composure remained complete; it was with an air of philosophic sadness rather than tempestuous grief that Elizabeth II accepted her destiny. She showed only one moment of animation, although so fleeting that many missed it, and that was in response to a shout from someone in the crowd outside the Abbey. Instead of the huzzas, the cheers and the 'Vivat Elizabethas' so carefully orchestrated by the new government, a voice had the temerity to call out: 'Long live the Protestant king over the border, long live King Charles.' Perhaps a tear shone in the new queen's eye. But Elizabeth II quickly recovered her melancholy composure; there was a scuffle and the audacious dissenter was dragged away by soldiers. The usual penalties for anti-government protest, the stocks and mutilation of the ears, were no doubt exacted.

The tragic air of Elizabeth Stuart, Queen of Great Britain, was hardly to be wondered at. For this scenario of her accession and coronation proposes that her father, mother and elder brother Henry, prince of Wales, as well as the preponderance of the nobility, higher clergy and many members of the House of

Commons had died in a colossal explosion at the opening of Parliament less than three months before, on 5 November 1605. Elizabeth, at the house of her governor the Lord Harington, Coombe Abbey in the Midlands near Rugby, had escaped the blast.

Of the surviving members of what had once been the most flourishing young royal family in recent British history, Elizabeth's younger sister Princess Mary, seven months old at the time of the disaster, was a delicate child who would in fact shortly succumb to one of the many common infant illnesses. Then there was Prince Charles, recently created duke of York, the usual title of the king's second son: under-sized, a late walker and talker, he was not yet five at the time of the explosion. Prince Charles had not in the end been at the opening of Parliament, although the possibility had been discussed. He had been considered too young and, frankly, too lacking in the kind of glamour which princes and princesses were supposed to display to impress the people with their favourite 'exterior shows'. It was Charles's elder brother Henry, prince of Wales, whose appearance, tall, handsome and martial, had incarnated everything a nation might hope for in its future ruler. Charles on the other hand was believed to be such a liability that he had only been brought down from Scotland to join his brother and sisters in late 1604, and then courtiers had not rushed to join the new royal household for fear the puny little prince would die and leave them stranded.

How ironic it was, then, that of King James's 'cubs', as he proudly called them, boasting happily of the royal nursery which the late Virgin Queen had never been able to provide, it was the despised Charles who had survived the blast, and that because of his own weakness. After that, Charles's destiny was to be strange indeed: rescued by loyal Scottish servants from the mayhem of Westminster, he was rushed north to the safety of

Scotland and there proclaimed king by the Scottish nobles, who were only too anxious to recover the independence they had so recently lost with the accession of their king to the mightier English throne.

In January 1606, in the immediate aftermath of the successful Gunpowder Plot, there were thus two sovereigns within the British Isles: one, nominally Catholic, at any rate heavily supported by Catholic France, Elizabeth II; the other, nominally Protestant or rather Calvinist, Charles I, upheld in Scotland and upheld by the Scottish nobility – for the time being without foreign support.

The Plot had its genesis in the despair in the hearts of the Catholic community after the new king, James I, had – in their view – broken the promises he made to them while in Scotland. The persecution of Catholics, involving fines, imprisonments, barbarously carried out deaths of priests, deaths for those who harboured priests, had been horribly severe in the last years of Elizabeth I's reign. The Mass itself was an illegal act, and the various other disabilities imposed upon Catholics for even the discreet practice of their religion make harrowing reading. It was on the Catholics that all men fastened their hatred, wrote a priest who was himself imprisoned in the Tower, Fr. William Weston: 'They lay in ambush for them, betrayed them, attacked them with violence and without warning. They plundered them at night, confiscated their possessions, drove away their flocks, stole their cattle.' In a way even more harrowing to devout Catholics was the fact that they were not allowed to baptize their children Catholics but were compelled to do so in a Protestant church, just as adults had to marry in a Protestant church. Protestant churchgoing on Sundays was also compulsory for fear of fines.

All this meant that the Catholic recusant population – the

word comes from refusal, the refusal of Catholics to attend Protestant services – had largely gone underground by the time Elizabeth I died. The head of the family and his male heir might profess the Protestant faith, to avoid fines and loss of properties, while the rest of the family, especially the mother, remained Catholic, carrying the torch forward to future generations in secret. In general, the Catholic women took advantage of their presumed weakness and virtually non-existent status at law, to protect priests and generally preserve the network of the faithful. People turned Catholic on their deathbeds when it could no longer damage them materially, having probably been Catholic in their hearts all along.

It was therefore especially significant in terms of the Gunpowder Plot (and its possible success) that no one really knew for sure, nor could know, how many Catholics there were in England in 1603 and whether their numbers would remain static in the months that followed. The Anglican bishops assured their new king at his accession that there were only 8,000 recusant adults, whereas it has been suggested that the true figure was more like 35,000. Three years later this figure was said to have risen to 100,000 under the comparatively mild regime with which James started – something which fatally aroused Catholic hopes before dashing them again with severer penalties. (As a contemporary percipiently observed of the Gunpowder Plot, 'hope deferred maketh the heart sick'.)

This emergence of the Catholics from the shadows did not pass without comment – hostile comment. In the words of Sir Henry Spiller in a speech in Parliament, 'The strength of the Catholic body, with the suspension of persecution, at once became evident.' Yet the idea of 65,000 adults becoming suddenly convinced of the truth of Catholic religion in a short space of time is evidently ludicrous. The true picture is of a large if unquantifiable body of people ready and willing to worship according to the faith of their Catholic ancestors, provided they could do so with impunity for their families and their properties. King James, following the (real-life) failure of the Plot, referred to the conspirators' vain hopes of a 'snowball' effect: they had been 'dreaming to themselves that they had the virtues of a snowball' which would begin in a small way, but by 'tumbling down from a great hill' would grow to an enormous size, 'gathering snow all the way'. But it was the fire of failure which melted the snowball; victory would surely have produced a very different result, with Catholics in large numbers coming out.

The basic elements of the Gunpowder Plot were as follows: a soldier of fortune named Guy Fawkes, a Catholic who had been serving in the (Spanish-ruled) Netherlands for some time and had indeed adopted the foreign version of his name, Guido, was brought back into his native country. This was for the purpose of placing an enormous quantity of gunpowder in the so-called 'cellar' of the House of Lords. The cellar was in fact on the ground floor rather than underground (as generations of myths about Fawkes as the sinister mole-in-the-black-vault would go on to pretend). Used sometimes for the coal and firewood needed for heating and cooking, it had also over the years accrued detritus such as pieces of masonry and was in general untidy and very dirty: in fact more of a storehouse than a cellar.

The cellar belonged to the house of one John Whynniard which lay conveniently enough right in the heart of Westminster, at right angles to the House of Lords, parallel to a short passage which was known as Parliament Place. This led on to Parliament Stairs, which gave access to the river some forty yards away. The cellar itself happened to be directly under the chamber of the House of Lords where the opening of Parliament was always held. It was rented in advance – without any difficulty at all – by one of the chief conspirators. This was

Thomas Percy, a kinsman of the powerful earl of Northumberland who had been involved in Catholic intrigues even before the accession of James I to the throne.

One should emphasize, odd as it may seem to a highly security-conscious age like our own, especially where the seat of government is concerned, that there was nothing at all odd about this rental; Thomas Percy simply explained that he needed additional accommodation for his servant with his wife in London, paid his £4 rental and that was that. Nor was the potentially lethal position of the cellar itself a problem. The palace of Westminster, at this date and for many years to come, was a warren of meeting-rooms, semi-private chambers and apartments as well as commercial enterprises of all sorts (as the diaries of Pepys sixty years later amply attest). Still less did the inhabitants of Westminster show any signs of recognizing the servant 'John Johnson' for what he was: a Catholic conspirator under an assumed identity. Fawkes had been abroad for some years and although the busy government intelligence service had his actual name in their sights, the connection was never made (in real life) until Fawkes himself confessed under torture.

Providing the gunpowder, at this period, was not a problem either, another pertinent if surprising fact. The government in theory had the monopoly but it meant little in practical terms when gunpowder was part of the equipment of every soldier, including the militia and trained bands, and every merchant vessel had a substantial stock. Proclamations from the government forbidding the selling-off of ordnance and munitions, including gunpowder, show how common the practice was. A total of thirty-six barrels were acquired without difficulty and introduced into the cellar by the easy river route. This was the common means of communication between the two banks of the Thames at this time, the chief conspirator Robert Catesby having his lodgings on the south side of the river. Although estimates of the amount of gunpowder have differed due to the many unreliable testimonies which followed the (real-life) dénouement, 10,000 pounds is the highest figure and 2,000 the lowest; no one has ever disputed that this was more than enough to blow the House of Lords and its wretched denizens sky-high.

A conveniently placed cellar, a huge quantity of explosive, an obscure conspirator ready to touch the fuse and then escape by the river: all these elements were well and truly in place in November 1605 with no particular reason why they should have been discovered before the big bang itself took place – had it not been for treachery by an insider. But of course no conspiracy of this sort exists in a vacuum and it was the motivation which was the crucial element here, bringing with it many complications including natural human resistance to the shedding of blood of innocent people for some higher cause.

The charismatic leader Robert Catesby, who had called his companions to a meeting in a London tavern in May 1604 with the words 'The nature of the disease requires so sharp a remedy', was by now in the Midlands. In Warwickshire and elsewhere – Shakespeare's country, remembering Shakespeare's own strong recusant origins – Catholic feeling had never been suppressed. It was probably the fine young horseman Sir Everard Digby, a familiar figure at the court, who was deputed to seize the Princess Elizabeth before proclaiming her queen and it was almost certainly the earl of Northumberland who was intended to act as her regent or Protector during her childhood.

Although nothing of this nature was ever proved against Northumberland and he was actually among those peers who attended the opening of Parliament, it was not for nothing that he was imprisoned subsequently in the Tower of London. Logic told the government that the conspirators must have had a prominent figure in mind to lead the regime in the name of Elizabeth (as Protector Somerset had done for the nine-year-old Edward VI). On the night of 4 November Northumberland, at his base near London at Syon House, suddenly announced that he was 'sleepy because of his early rising that day' and would not attend. It is true that this spasm of fatigue – if it was fatigue and not self-preservation – passed; but the fact that Northumberland changed his mind yet again and did attend may have been due to someone tipping him off that (in real life) the gunpowder had been discovered in the vaults and removed . . . in which case Northumberland needed to act quickly in order to establish his innocence.

So far there was nothing in the Plot itself which guaranteed failure – and with its sheer daring, there was a great hope of a triumphant if gruesome success. The human element which led to the discovery a few days in advance of the intended explosion was the mixed reaction of Lord Monteagle to the news of what was intended. He was probably informed of what was planned by one of the conspirators, his brother-in-law Francis Tresham. Monteagle on the one hand revolted at the thought of the deaths of the innocent and on the other hand saw a splendid opportunity for personal advancement by warning the Chief Minister Salisbury (and the king) of what was threatening. There have been many proposed explanations of the anonymous Monteagle letter, which was delivered in a suitably mysterious fashion under cover of darkness. It began: 'My Lord . . . devise some excuse to shift of your attendance at this Parliament . . . For though there be no appearance of any stir, yet I say they shall receive a terrible blow this Parliament and yet they shall not see who hurts them . . .' However, the obvious theory, that Monteagle wrote it himself, is not easily contradicted, since he was the enormous beneficiary of the whole business. If Monteagle had not succumbed to the temptation of treachery for a mixture of motives, noble and material, there is no reason to suppose that the Plot would have been detected in advance.

Let us suppose, then, that the Gunpowder Plot, with its avowed aim of ending the persecution of the Catholics, is successful in nearly all its elements – with one tiny failure or rather bungle, seemingly unimportant in the general confusion (and conspiratorial rejoicing) but with, it is suggested, momentous consequences. The plotters had never really grappled with the question of little Prince Charles, the runt of the litter who had arrived so late on the royal family scene. After assuming that he would attend the House of Lords like his elder brother, they had vaguely considered abducting him if he did not. Subsequent to the discovery of the Plot one of Prince Charles's servants deposed that Thomas Percy had come to the little prince's lodgings and 'made enquiries as to the way into his chamber' and 'where he rode abroad' and with how many attendants. What Percy might have contemplated could, however, easily have been carried out in the immediate aftermath of the explosion by some of the many loyal Scots who had come south with the prince's father.

The notion of Prince Charles being proclaimed king of Scotland (he was after all by royal rules the rightful heir after the deaths of James and Henry, having precedence as a male over his older sister) and educated as a Calvinist, as James had been with stern tutors, is perfectly plausible. His childhood would indeed have had remarkable parallels with that of the young James, ruler from an even younger age, with a series of regents. Many royal children in history had to endure new religious orientations which may have been originally unwelcome (although at under five, and being backward, Charles would not have suffered as much as Elizabeth, already at nine publicly pious as well as Protestant).

I shall return to the question of how the future of King Charles I of Scotland and Queen Elizabeth II of England might have worked out in the years to come. But in the meantime what of England? It is now that the issue of foreign support or the lack of it becomes crucial. The two most powerful European countries – France and Spain – were both Catholic, Henri IV of France having converted from Protestantism twelve years earlier in order to ascend the throne, with the celebrated quip: 'Paris is worth a Mass'. Spain in addition ruled the so-called Spanish Netherlands, an area that very roughly approximated to modern Belgium, in the persons of the joint governors, 'the Archdukes', as the married couple were known, Albert and Isabella, respectively nephew and daughter of the king of Spain.

Although in real life all the Catholic powers, including the Pope himself, hastened to express absolute horror at the devilish conspiracy which had been planned, a different result might have brought very different reactions. Northumberland's regime (he was not technically a Catholic, although obviously he had strong Catholic sympathies) might have concentrated on binding manifest wounds. With the spirit of the shared religious past invoked he might have attempted to unite loyal Anglicans and Catholics, with persecution for the latter of course ended. (Puritans would have been another matter and would surely have looked yearningly towards Scotland.) Under the circumstances Spain, which had actually cooled on supporting yet another attempt at invasion on behalf of the English Catholics, taking part in a treaty with James I in 1604, might have discovered very different sympathies in the interests of realpolitik. Spain would certainly not have contemplated an invasion on behalf of the English Protestant interest and it may be that the supportive troops from Spanish Flanders, on which the conspirators (remembering Guy Fawkes had served there) pinned such hopes, would actually have arrived.

Still less would the France of the ultra-pragmatic Henri IV have refrained from trying to win the new game of alliances. The researches of John Bossy have shown that around the turn of the seventeenth century France took a new interest in the plight of the English Catholics, attempting (not with total success) to sort the internal disputes between the Jesuits and the so-called Appellants, priests who were more accommodating with the civil order. There were connections there already and it is difficult to believe that Henri IV would not have played the game to the top of its bent.

At quite a different level, that of matrimonial alliances, one of the French princes was an obvious husband for the new Queen Elizabeth, since the question of Henri's eldest son and the then princess had already been discussed favourably in the lifetime of her father. James had boasted to the French ambassador that his 'Bessy' was already quite enamoured of the dauphin's portrait. (Elizabeth II, in her revolutionized new life, would at least have been able to comfort herself with that memory.) There had also been some question of a double marriage, despite the difference in religion, with Prince Henry marrying the eldest daughter of France; during his brief lifetime Henry had promised his beloved sister that he would not consent to this unless she duly became dauphiness. Marie de Médicis and Henri IV had three sons in all, and if marrying the dauphin (the future Louis XIII) to the queen of England was now considered altogether too ambitious a project, a combination of the two thrones likely to enrage European opinion, then the conventional route would be to marry a younger French prince to Elizabeth II (as the duc d'Alençon had been suggested as a bridegroom for her great predecessor).

While this prospect of an Anglo-French closeness is merely

sketched in, it would be a conciliatory and practical route for the new government to take. France (and Henri IV) had plenty of understanding of the problem of religious minorities with its sizeable Huguenot population, to which Henri had once belonged. All of this is to suggest that the frightful atrocity – as it would have been – of an explosion killing off most of the English establishment would not in fact have resulted in a foreign invasion. After all, who would have invaded and to what end? On the contrary, the great powers, as great powers always have, would have searched for an accommodation which was to their own advantage.

It remains to hope that the imaginary reign of Queen Elizabeth II would have been marked by more tolerance towards the Puritan dissident sects than that of the first Elizabeth towards the Catholics. Certainly the young Elizabeth Stuart would have made an excellent queen, with her intelligence, charm and sense of ceremonial which she had already displayed at the tender age of nine. In real life, she has been known to history as the Winter Queen, or Elizabeth of Bohemia, from the short-lived reign there of her husband Frederick, prince of the Palatine. In the adversities which followed the rapid dispossession of the young couple, Elizabeth always displayed remarkable strength of character. She was also blessed with remarkable fertility, giving birth to a huge and vigorous family of thirteen children including the soldier prince Rupert of the Rhine and the princess Sophia whose descendants, the Hanoverians, still sit today on the British throne. While one cannot extrapolate the course of one marriage with a completely different man from another, there is reason to hope that the Anglo-French marriage of Elizabeth and a Bourbon prince would have resulted in a similar proliferation of heirs.

That is the optimistic prognosis to the success of the Gunpowder Plot. Alternatively one could argue more pessimistically that there is an inexorable beat to the march of history. With religious strife continuing in England between Catholics and High Church Anglicans, and Puritans, coupled with the (legitimate) dynastic claims to the English throne of the young Scottish king, Charles, one can easily envisage hostilities between the two countries escalating. There might have been a war in, say, 1639 (the date in real life of the first Anglo-Scottish so-called Bishops' war) . . . Perhaps after all fate is not so easily outwitted. Let us go further and imagine King Charles captured, tried, and the warrant for his execution signed by his unwilling – but in the end royally ruthless – sister, Queen Elizabeth II, on 30 January 1649 . . .

And the rhyme the children would sing around the bonfire?

> Please to remember the Fifth of November,
> Gunpowder Freedom and Plot.
> We know no reason why Gunpowder Freedom
> Should ever be forgot.

Of course they ask for a penny for (King) Jamie, not the Guy.

CHAPTER THREE

Four Hundred Years of Festivities

DAVID CRESSY

Unlike new nations that celebrate their independence, or old nations that commemorate their revolutions, the English observe no national anniversary to focus and express their patriotism. St George's Day is virtually meaningless; the queen's birthday has limited appeal; and none of the great national victories, from Agincourt to the Armada, from Trafalgar to the Battle of Britain, operates in the calendar or in consciousness like the Fourth of July in America or the Fourteenth of July in France. Much of the festive energy available for such occasions has been devoted, instead, to commemorations of the Fifth of November.

Of all historical providences engrained in the memory of English Protestants, the discovery of the Gunpowder Plot on the eve of 5 November 1605 was the most enduring. Other events of the Tudor and Stuart period may have been more important, but the story of Guy Fawkes's attempt to blow up king and Parliament with gunpowder was most widely and systematically remembered. The annual celebration of its defeat enlivened autumns from the Jacobean period to the Victorian. In an attenuated form we remember it still.

Everyone raised in England knows the rhyme, 'Please to remember the Fifth of November,/Gunpowder Treason and Plot. We know no reason why Gunpowder Treason/Should ever be forgot.' And an older generation may recall the more aggressive alternative, 'Penny for the Guy,/Hit him in the eye,/Stick him up

49

Guy Vaux the 2ᵈ. 54

The Wicked is Snared in the Work
of his own Hands thou hast
seen it — Psalm 10ᵗʰ

a lamp-post [or chimney]/And there let him die.' For 400 years the English have commemorated the unsuccessful attempt by Guy Fawkes and his associates to blow up the Houses of Parliament. And in the twenty-first century we still celebrate Guy Fawkes Night or Bonfire Night with fireworks and bonfires, ritualized begging, charitable collecting, costuming, masking, mischief, the burning of effigies and the recitation of doggerel verse. The character of the celebration may have shifted from religious exaltation to rowdy disturbances, from ruffians' activity to quaint English custom, but the commemorative action endures.

A series of questions springs to mind, and this essay begins to explore some of them. Why is the only annual firework celebration in the English popular calendar associated with the collapse of a seventeenth-century Roman Catholic conspiracy? What does the commemoration mean, and what different meanings have attached to it in the past? What kind of memory has been perpetuated, through what processes and for what purposes? What was the role played by Church and state, political parties and radical groups, newspapers and community organizations, in orchestrating and interpreting the celebration? When did the various names for the anniversary – 'Gunpowder Treason Day', 'Guy Fawkes Night', 'Firework Night', etc. – come into use, and what cultural and political freight did they carry? How was a highly charged national Protestant calendrical memory created in the seventeenth century, and how has it been sustained, manipulated, altered and appropriated, between the Jacobean period and the present? How deeply embedded was the memory of 1605, and to what degree were the commemorations self-consciously 'kept up'? To what extent did the Gunpowder Plot commemoration create a common and cohesive festival that gave unity to English popular culture, and to what degree was it used, by contrast, to express sectional, partisan, political, social and confessional antagonisms? Was it, in its Victorian manifestation, an exclusively local opportunity for a rough plebeian charivari, or was it still influenced by national debates about politics and religion? Whose festival was it, and where is it situated in the interplay between elite and popular cultures?

Much speculative nonsense has been written about the bonfire traditions that developed around the anniversary of the Gunpowder Plot on 5 November. Folklorists, anthropologists and historians have often claimed that Guy Fawkes Night is a secular replacement of the ancient Celtic and Nordic fire festivals of Samhain or *nod-fyr* (need-fire). The medieval Church absorbed these pagan festivals and transformed them into the Christian holy days of the Eve of All-Hallows (Hallowe'en) and All Souls' Day. But much of the pre-Christian meaning is said to have lingered in an attenuated form. Besides its nominal religious content, the occasion stood out as a harvest festival and a marker of the end of summer, when there might be debris or surplus materials to burn. Bonfires were lit, it is believed, to strengthen the power of the waning sun. With the decay of All-Hallows in England after the Reformation, the argument continues, the people found it convenient to transfer their festivity (and their fires) to the newly appointed Gunpowder Treason Day.

The folkloric theory, set forth under the influence of Sir James Frazer's *Golden Bough*, was that 'Guy Fawkes Night' exemplified 'the recrudescence of old customs in modern shapes'. It was 'a decadent survival' with 'maimed rites' of an ancient agricultural festival that was taken over for 'ecclesiastico-political' purposes in the seventeenth century. Modern celebrations of the Fifth of November in South Yorkshire, Lancashire and Derbyshire are supposedly linked to 'an old feast held in honour of the Scandinavian god Thor'. Some folklorists have even suggested that the burning of Guy Fawkes in effigy was 'the commemoration of a pre-Christian human sacrifice', a remnant of an ancient primitive religion.

The first part of the story is doubtless true. Given the propensity in human culture to adapt existing materials, the claim that an ancient autumn festival lies behind the Christian observances of All-Hallows has strong plausibility. But there is no historical evidence to support the notion that Guy Fawkes Night shares these origins. The choice of 5 November for Gunpowder Treason Day comes from the timing of the opening of Parliament and the discovery of the Gunpowder Plot, and had nothing to do with the continuing observance of ancient fire festivals. There is barely a flicker of evidence for autumn fires in England at the beginning of the seventeenth century; and although eighteenth- and nineteenth-century observers could point to rustic practices involving ritual fires at this time of year, the evidence is unclear as to whether these were survival, revival or invention. Further suspicions are aroused by the observation that most of these bonfires were reported from the Celtic fringe or the north and west, whereas the Guy Fawkes–Gunpowder Plot commemorations took strongest root in the south and east.

It is, of course, possible that the Gunpowder Treason observances triggered a synapse in the English folk memory, and that they may have sounded echoes of a lost or vestigial tradition. But without evidence we cannot support this conclusion. It is more likely that the 5 November bonfires involved the application of an established festive form (the celebratory bonfire) to a new festive occasion sponsored by the state. The burning of effigies (of popes and devils, not of Guy Fawkes) was unknown to the first generation of the Stuart era and was rare before the 1670s; it owes nothing to a putative heritage of human sacrifices. The origins of the festival can be found in the

1606 Act of Parliament, and in the Elizabethan and Jacobean tradition of politicized bell-ringing and celebration. European Renaissance societies lit bonfires as *feux de joi*, to celebrate royal births and marriages, victories and homecomings. They lit them too at midsummer, at midwinter and on holy days, as expressions of joy and gratulation. Protestant England adapted this custom to its particular religious and dynastic celebrations.

In 1605 a group of Catholic gentlemen hatched a desperate plot to kill King James and to overthrow the Protestant regime. The government learned of the plot, and found Guy Fawkes – the man with the match – in the cellars at Westminster with thirty-six barrels of gunpowder. The conspirators were rounded up, tortured and executed. All credit for the discovery was given to God. Parliament passed 'An act for a public thanksgiving to Almighty God every year on the fifth day of November ... to the end this unfained thankfulness may never be forgotten, but be had in perpetual remembrance'. This is one of the earliest examples of legislated memory, and it provided a model for subsequent acts of commemoration.

The preamble to the legislation lays out the official interpretation:

Forasmuch as almighty God hath in all ages showed his power and mercy in the miraculous and gracious deliverance of his church, and in the protection of religious kings and states, and that no nation of the earth hath been blessed with greater benefit than this kingdom now enjoyeth, having the true and free profession of the gospel under our most gracious sovereign lord King James, the most great learned and religious king that ever reigned therein, enriched with a most hopeful and plentiful progeny proceeding out of his royal loins promising continuance of this happiness and profession to all posterity: the which many malignant and devilish papists, Jesuits, and seminary priests much envying and fearing, conspired most horribly, when the king's most excellent majesty, the queen, the prince, and the lords spiritual and temporal, and commons, should have been assembled in the upper house of Parliament upon the fifth day of November in the year of our lord 1605 suddenly to have blown up the said whole house with gunpowder; an invention so inhuman, barbarous and cruel, as the like was never before heard of.

Special prayers were written, appealing to the 'Lord, who didst this day discover the snares of death that were laid for us, and didst wonderfully deliver us from the same, be thou still our mighty protector, and scatter our enemies that delight in blood. Infatuate and defeat their counsels, abate their pride, assuage their malice, and counfound their devices.' Most parishes purchased the *Form of Prayer with Thanksgiving to be used yearly upon the Fifth day of November: For the happy Deliuerance of the King, and the Three Estates of the Realm, from the most Traiterous and bloody intended Massacre by Gun-powder.* These anti-Catholic sentiments – a curse as much as a prayer – remained in the Church of England service book until 1859.

To Jacobean divines the discovery of the plot was a wonderful providence, a confirmation of God's covenant with England and an endorsement of the Protestant Stuart dynasty. Remembering it helped to solidify their sense of the English as a chosen people. Bishop Lancelot Andrewes preached at court on the first anniversary, 'this day of ours, this fifth of November, a day of God's making . . . is the Scripture fulfilled in our ears . . . the destroyer passed over our dwellings this day. It is our Passover, it is our Purim.' It was also an occasion for anti-Catholic vindictiveness and patriotic merry-making. As far as Church and state were concerned, the Gunpowder Plot should be remembered for ever.

The physician Francis Herring's remarks were typical: 'The

Powder-treason, that monstrous birth of the Romish harlot, cannot be forgotten without great impiety and injury to ourselves . . . We shall be guilty of horrible ingratitude, the foulest of all vices, if we do not embrace all means of perpetuating the memory of so great, so gracious, and wonderful a preservation.' The plot represented 'the quintessence of Satan's policy, the furthest reach and stain of human malice and cruelty, not to be parallelled among the savage Turks, the barbarous Indians, nor, as I am persuaded, among the more brutish cannibals'. Latin poets like John Milton punned on the quintessence of cruelty, 'in quintum Novembris'.

George Carleton, James I's bishop of Chichester, explained the diabolical comprehensiveness of the Gunpowder plotters.

Their hellish device was at one blow to root out religion, to destroy the state, the father of our country, the mother of our country, the olive branches the hopeful succession of our king, the reverend clergy, the honorable nobility, the faithful councillors, the grave judges, the greatest part of our knights and gentry, the choicest burgesses, the officers of the crown, council, signet, seals, and other seats of judgement, the learned lawyers, with an infinite number of common people, the hall of justice, the houses of parliament, the church used for the coronation of our kings, the monuments of our former princes, all records of parliament, and of every particular man's right, with great number of charters, and other things of this nature, all these things had the devil by his agents devised at one secret blow to destroy.

Their failure was a cause for perpetual rejoicing. Almanacs, histories, litanies and sermons, as well as the ritual celebration of bonfires and bells, helped imprint the memory of the Gunpowder Plot on the English popular consciousness. The commemoration was an act of loyalty as well as piety, with national, dynastic and religious connotations. Many parishes heard sermons on 5 November, and many more augmented the commemoration with public drinking or solemn processions. In some towns, such as Canterbury and Norwich, the celebration of the Fifth of November displayed much of the festive energy that before the Reformation had been reserved for saints' days. The anniversary became a day of indulgence, of drinking and festivity as well as worship and meditation, even though it was never an official day of absence from work.

After 1618 renewed concerns about Catholicism, anxieties about James's pro-Spanish foreign policy and alarm that international Protestantism was in retreat led to sermons calling for greater solemnity and more profound thanksgiving each 5 November. Radical Puritans like Thomas Hooker and moderate episcopalians like George Carleton agreed on the significance of the Fifth of November and the duty of holding it in memory. The opening of Charles I's reign and the renewal of hostilities with Spain saw a remarkable unity among English Protestants which became especially manifest on Gunpowder Treason Day. Parish observances, both festive and solemn, united centre and localities, court and country, in a common patriotic occasion.

But the Gunpowder Treason anniversary soon lost its unifying character and took on an increasingly partisan tone. In the 1630s Charles I, married to a Catholic, found the anti-papist bonfires distasteful, and sought to muffle the commemoration. The Arminian ceremonialists who rose in the Church preferred the old calendar of saints' days to the newer cycle of Protestant deliverances. All of this – plus restored altars, slack sabbaths, and rigid discipline – threw Puritan preachers on to the defensive, and some of them retaliated by re-emphasizing and re-interpreting the Fifth of November. Radicals like the London minister Henry Burton used the anniversary to challenge what they saw as creeping popery, and to stress the need for further reformation.

Burton explained, in the printed version of his sermons, 'I deemed that day, the memorial whereof should cause all loyal subjects forever to detest all innovations tending to reduce us to that religion of Rome, which plotted matchless treason, the most seasonable for this text . . . This is a time of sorrow and humiliation, but this day a day of joy and festivity.' It was time, on 5 November 1636, to recall the true meaning of the deliverance from the Gunpowder Plot, 'a deliverance never to be cancelled out of the calendar, but to be written in every man's heart forever'. Formidable collisions took place over the interpretation of the Fifth of November, and Burton's sermon brought him before the High Commission and to the pillory, where he lost a portion of his ears.

In the revolutionary decade of the 1640s the Gunpowder commemoration became charged with new significance as fresh conspiracies were feared or uncovered. Parliamentary sermons on 5 November blended historical and biblical reminiscence with calls to action in England's continuing emergency. Preaching before the House of Commons on 5 November 1644, Charles Herle spoke as if he were preparing the members for combat: 'You must expect to stand in need of more deliverances: the same brood of enemies that then durst venture but an undermining, dare now attempt an open battery.' The Philistine pioneers were tunnelling 'from Oxford, Rome, Hell, to Westminster, and there to blow up, if possible, the better foundations of your houses, their liberties and privileges'. Parliamentarians took possession of the November anniversary, though Royalists disputed their interpretation.

Some features of the Gunpowder commemoration were neglected or suppressed in the revolutionary 1650s. There was awkwardness and uncertainty as to whether the republican regime should commemorate a Stuart dynastic deliverance. But most parishes still rang their bells each 5 November, and preachers adapted their anniversary sermons to the changing conditions. Unofficially, the day was marked by the lighting of bonfires and the exploding of squibs and crackers. On the night of 5 November 1657 the Master of Jesus College, Cambridge, was greeted by a gunpowder squib thrown through his window, by no means the last fireworks disturbance in the university town.

Writing during Oliver Cromwell's Protectorate, Samuel Clarke shared the determination that Gunpowder Treason should never be forgotten. He wrote to the end 'that all sorts may be stirred up to real thankfulness and transmit the same to their posterity; that their children may know the reason why the fifth of November is celebrated; that God may have glory, and the papists perpetual infamy'. Clarke rehearsed the narrative of the plot 'lest the remembrance of so signal a mercy and deliverance, vouchsafed by God both to our church and state, should be buried in oblivion'.

But any danger that the anniversary might lapse into oblivion was soon overcome by its continuing utility for religious polemic and political mobilization. Formal observance of the Gunpowder Plot was fully reinstated with the Restoration. The annual thanksgiving was still enjoined by statute, and provided a model for the two new statutory anniversaries of 30 January and 29 May – the one for the execution of Charles, king and martyr; the other for the restoration of his son, the May King, on Royal Oak Day. Officially, 5 November marked the preservation of king and Church, and was honoured in these terms by courtiers, high Anglicans and Tories. But in Charles II's reign the anniversary took on alternative and oppositional meanings. By this time the memory of 1605 belonged to political culture at large, and could not be controlled by any one interest.

By the 1670s London apprentices were turning 5 November

into a dramatic anti-Catholic fire festival, as well as a challenge to sobriety and good order. They stopped coaches and demanded money for alcohol and bonfires. And in 1673 they paraded an effigy of the Whore of Babylon, decked out with 'all the whorish ornaments' of papal crosses, keys, beads and triple crown, and carried it in a torchlight procession to 'a great bonfire' in the Poultry. Before this date we hear little about the burning of effigies on 5 November, but henceforth they would be a standard feature of the commemoration. Anti-Catholic processions and demonstrations featured effigies of the Pope, his minions, and figures from English history.

At the height of the Popish Plot and the Exclusion struggle the Whig opposition orchestrated elaborate pope-burning processions, while the mob engaged in battles over bonfires and drunken attacks on Catholics' houses. The organized pageantry even had its own souvenir programmes, such as *The manner of the Burning of the Pope in Effigies in London On the 5th of November, 1678, With the manner of carrying him through several Streets, in progression to Temple-Bar, where at length he was decently burned*. Publications of this sort commemorated the commemoration, and reconnected the spectacle of the street with the political discourse of print. The anniversary became politicized, a point of division between Whigs and Tories. And at the same time it was acquiring a folk life of its own, with a vocabulary of symbolic action – including burning effigies and breaking windows – that was barely controlled by the parliamentary elite.

The accession of a Catholic king in 1685 gave an ironic twist to the observance of anti-Catholic anniversaries. James II's government banned fireworks and tried to limit celebrations, but most parishes kept up their traditions of bell-ringing, sermons and bonfires. And after 1688 the anniversary of the landing of William of Orange – significantly but fortuitously on

5 November – focused attention on the double deliverance of liberty and religion. Celebrations of William's birthday on 4 November became entwined with commemorations of his landing on the 5th. In a further mutation, the Gunpowder anniversary was harnessed to the struggle against arbitrary government and Jacobite tyranny, as well as popish religion.

By the end of the Stuart period the Gunpowder anniversary had become a polysemous occasion, replete with polyvalent cross-referencing, meaning all things to all men. In the calendar of court and Parliament it was a day of thanksgiving and prayer, with appropriate appearances and feasting; the legislation of 1605 was still in force, and ministers recited the prayers calling God to scatter England's enemies. High Anglicans used the occasion to recall God's blessings on the established Church and to warn of the danger from dissenters; others warned of the continuing danger from Rome; Jacobites raised glasses to the Stuart dynasty, recalling the deliverances of 1605 and 1660; the Whigs made 5 November a holiday to enjoy the blessings of the revolution. And below the level of the politically and religiously engaged elite, common people in town and country lit bonfires and threw fireworks, drank heavily and settled their own scores under the cover of England's unique anniversary.

During most of the eighteenth century the courtly, parliamentary and civic observances of the Gunpowder Plot were dutiful but muted. Customary routine preserved the Fifth of November as a 'holiday at all the public offices', but much of the fire had gone out of it, as just one among forty-nine official holidays. The new Hanoverian elite had diminishing interest in seventeenth-century religious deliverances, so long as Church and state were secure. As far as high society and high politics were concerned in Walpole's time, the Gunpowder anniversary had shed most of its meaning. Whigs might still reflect on the liberties that were secured on 5 November, though they were more inclined to remember 1688 than 1605; Tories might still recall dynastic history and the salvation of the Church of England. But public attention was directed towards formulaic observance, rather than impassioned political or religious memory. Were it not for the service books and the almanac, it is possible that Gunpowder Treason would have been forgot.

Eighteenth-century almanacs continued to mark the day in red letters, but with more respect to antiquarian than to present concerns (almanacs were often the most archaic of publications). Often the Gunpowder anniversary became submerged beneath other, current enthusiasms that adopted a similar vocabulary of celebration. In 1741, for example, the *Gentleman's Magazine* reported no domestic occurrences on 5 November, but the following Thursday, 'being the birthday of Admiral Vernon, was distinguished with ringing of bells, bonfires, and illuminations in the cities of London and Westminster, Liverpool, etc.'. The Fifth of November observances in the 1760s were overshadowed by John Wilkes's birthday on 28 October, the duke of Cumberland's birthday on 7 November, and by the ceremonies for the Lord Mayor's Day or the opening of Parliament. *An Almanac for . . . 1775* showed thirteen red-letter days in November, including the birthdays of Prince Edward, the duke of Cumberland, the Princess Sophia Augusta and the duke of Gloucester, as well as the day of the 'Papists Conspiracy'.

In most years under George II and George III the anniversary thanksgiving was observed with no more than 'the usual solemnity'; the Park and Tower guns were fired, and the evening concluded with 'bonfires, illuminations, ringing of bells' and fireworks on the river. Gunpowder Treason had become a state-sponsored spectacle, a polite entertainment rather than an occasion for vitriolic thanksgiving. Only in 1745, with the

Jacobite Rebellion, did 5 November resume its old flavour of mockery, defiance and religious venom.

Below the level of the elite, however, other groups invested the anniversary with social and political meanings of their own. Class hostilities took cultural form, as the Gunpowder commemoration developed into a festival of order against disorder, of respectability against misrule. The Fifth of November provided an annual occasion for the contest between rowdiness and discipline, a ritualized challenge to hierarchical power, in which the events of 1605 were largely forgotten. It barely mattered that Guy Fawkes had been a Catholic, or that the conspirators had tried to blow up Parliament. Now the historical anniversary served as a pretext for violence, a cover for challenges to the established order. Establishment politicians withdrew their sponsorship leaving young working men in temporary possession of the streets.

Newspapers complained of outrages and affronts to civility, though from different perspectives the same behaviour might be seen as cheerful good-fellowship and letting off of steam, or the articulation of class antagonisms. Enthusiasts lit bonfires in defiance of local authorities, and celebrants enlivened firework displays by throwing 'serpents', squibs and crackers among the crowd. Masked revellers ran wild and revenged themselves on unpopular or uncharitable neighbours by breaking windows and burning fences. It was time for settling scores, whether personal or socio-economic.

On 5 November 1766 'a dreadful fire broke out at Kettering in Northamptonshire, occasioned by the boys throwing squibs ... The common people, instead of joining to extinguish the flames, called out tauntingly to a farmer whose ricks were on fire, "Now, farmer, will you sell your wheat at seven and sixpence a strike?" ' Almost a century later the mob at Guildford asserted a different moral economy by making their Guy

Fawkes bonfire from the palings of a sports-ground proprietor who charged too much for admission.

On Gunpowder Night in the late eighteenth century 'greasy rogues' intimidated politer Londoners, and bonfire boys dunned passers-by for money. Youths outraged their elders and 'roughs' and 'ruffians' menaced householders in other towns. Respectable tradesmen complained of 'the swarm of boys' who extracted contributions, and solid citizens braced against the depredations of 'blackguards' and pickpockets. Mobs of 'idle fellows' caused 'great annoyance' to 'the public' and to the magistrates who feared their 'depredations and disorders' as artisans and apprentices took temporary possession of the streets. (The middle-class writers who provided these newspaper accounts had no doubts about their own socio-cultural affiliations.)

For both children and adults, the anniversary of the Gunpowder Plot provided a temporary privileged arena in which ordinary standards of lawfulness and civility could be set aside. It was commonly believed that reciting the verses for 5 November – 'please to remember' – licensed the bullying of passers-by into giving money. Wood could be stolen, fences broken down, so long as it became fuel for the bonfire. In some country parishes, villagers claimed the right to hunt over private ground on 5 November. Magistrates and property-owners disagreed.

In 1785 the traditional bonfire celebration at Lewes in Sussex degenerated into a riot and severely divided the community. 'Wicked, obstinate and malicious persons' alarmed 'the principal inhabitants' of Arlesford on that same 5 November 1785, when 'a lawless mob ... pelted the Justice and constables with stones, brickbats and sticks'. Only the fortitude of the magistrate, bailiff and principal inhabitants, so it was claimed, prevented 'a dangerous insurrection'.

The social challenge of Guy Fawkes Night continued into the

nineteenth century. 'Ruffianism, theft, and riotous conduct' were standard features of the Dickensian Fifth of November. A correspondent from Lewes complained in 1847 of 'the grossest riots and excess' that took over the town each year. 'Ruffians' intimidated respectable householders. 'Bonfire boys' in masks and 'fantastical dress' and armed with bats and bludgeons rolled lighted tar barrels through the streets. Lewes took Guy Fawkes Night seriously, and its annual bonfires were long believed to have been lit 'from time immemorial'. But other towns, especially in southern England, developed equally vigorous traditions. At Guildford gangs of bonfire celebrants calling themselves 'guys' put the town under siege during their Fifth of November 'lark'. 'Respectable tradesmen' and 'peaceable inhabitants' barred their doors against 'facetious rustics' and the menacing 'guys' during these annual 'riotous proceedings'. The immediate memory centred on local grudges, excess and damage, rather than historical or ideological recollections.

Guy Fawkes himself had always featured in the narrative of the Gunpowder Plot, but during the seventeenth century when it came to parading and burning effigies the figure of Guy was upstaged by the Pope and the devil. By the end of the eighteenth century, however, Guy Fawkes had emerged as the principal figure to be displayed and burned in effigy; and early in the nineteenth century Gunpowder Treason Day became 'Guy Fawkes Night', informally renamed in his honour. By the accession of Queen Victoria the autumn fire festival was invariably known as 'Guy Fawkes Night', and twentieth-century folklorists seem not to know it as anything else.

The Times reported in 1788 that 'Guy Faux in his usual state was carried about the streets in commemoration of the gunpowder plot.' In 1790 the newspaper mentioned boys 'begging for money to burn Guy Faux'. In 1792 'Guy Faux was burned by the populace', and so on. The desperado with the tall hat and dark lantern (both objects now on view at Oxford's Ashmolean museum), became a familiar figure on the autumn streets and in country towns and villages. William Cobbett, on his rural ride through Kent, remarked on the annual burning of 'Guy Fawkes, the pope and the devil'. As anti-Catholic agitation and historical memory subsided, Guy Fawkes took on the roles of all-purpose bogeyman and carnival grotesque. Children made their own versions with rags and paper (as they do today), but early Victorian technology inspired novel representations. In 1839 *The Times* reported: 'A machine twelve feet in height, constructed with tissue, filled with hydrogen gas, and representing the figure of Guy Fawkes ... rose in a perpendicular manner' over Pentonville and drifted south over the City. It was last seen heading across the river towards Kent.

A recurrent refrain in the nineteenth century was that the celebration of the Gunpowder Plot had declined. From time to time throughout Victoria's reign the newspapers claimed that the bonfire festivity no longer matched the livelier celebrations of yesteryear. Without ideological passion or organized force to drive it, the annual commemoration was indifferently 'kept up'. In 1834 *The Times* noted that the 'fiery zeal' of the Fifth of November had 'gradually decreased, and neither men nor boys any longer take a part or interest in such observance of the day'. The Gunpowder Plot had lost its religious and patriotic meaning, 'and children carry about their "poor Guy" with no other sentiment or knowledge respecting him than that his exhibition procures them a few pence'. A magistrate who dealt with a Guy Fawkes Night affray in 1839 'said, he thought the day was almost forgotten'. In 1843 a correspondent wrote that 'the observance of the fifth of November has been considerably on the decline for some time'. Even the association of Guy

Fawkes 'with little boys and fireworks . . . has subsided of late'. In 1850 *The Times* described the anniversary as 'of late years almost forgotten'. Again in the 1860s the occasion was 'but indifferently observed'. The anniversary 'passed off very tamely' in 1877, and *The Times* remarked on the tameness of Guy Fawkes Night in each of the next few years. Activities on 5 November 1882 were lamentably 'of the tamest kind', with 'few grown lads or adults' taking part. By 1884 it appeared that 'the observance of the day' in London was 'gradually dying out'. In fact, Gunpowder Treason Day was changing again, not dying, and its apparent subsidence or tameness reflected other Victorian trends.

Revived religious antagonisms lent new power to the Gunpowder anniversary as Irish Catholics settled among Protestant Londoners. Guy Fawkes provided a mask for ethnic, social and religious confrontations. In 1838

the effigy of Guy Fawkes was carried by some boys followed by a crowd of others into a court inhabited chiefly by Irish coal-whippers and ballast-getters; who taking umbrage at the appearance of the effigy, and the shouts of the children calling out 'No popes' and 'Pray remember the fifth of November', were attacked by a number of Irish boys, who captured poor Guy and carried him off in triumph. The protestant boys obtained a reinforcement and made an attack on the 'Popes', as they called the catholic boys, and succeeded in regaining the effigy. The two parties commenced flinging stones at each other.

And later in the Victorian era there would again be affrays involving Irish labourers and a belligerent 'party with Guys'. Whether these collisions were more acute in areas like Liverpool has yet to be examined.

Catholic emancipation in 1829 and the advance of 'the Popish interest' in early Victorian politics also redirected attention to older religious issues. Conservative ministers took to their pulpits and made sure that the anti-Catholic service for the Fifth of November was vigorously observed. Popular histories revived the story of Guy Fawkes and the Gunpowder Treason. The call in the 1830s to 'Prefer the religion of the Bible to the blasphemies of the Vatican' echoed confessional tensions of the seventeenth century. But it is a mark of the diminution of religious conflict that when in 1833 the Houses of Parliament actually burned down, by accident, there was no rush to blame the Catholics, and no explicit association of the disaster with the Gunpowder Plot.

The re-establishment of a Catholic hierarchy and the revival of papal dignities in England in 1850 triggered a fresh round of Protestant sermons on the 'errors of popery' and the 'aggressions of Rome'. Conservative Anglicans lent support to popular radical opinion, as local and national issues intertwined. Anti-Catholic demonstrators took to the streets on 5 November with placards proclaiming 'no wafer gods' and 'no catholic humbug'. The 'Papal Aggression' of 1850 sparked firework disturbances at Towcester, Kettering and Northampton. Opposition to the Roman revival produced an elaborate anti-Catholic pageant and bonfire in the cathedral yard at Exeter, where figures of the Pope and his officers were consigned to the flames. Elsewhere in England, 'the bonfires were double in number and more than double in size those of former years'. Old men remarked that they had never seen such a Fifth of November as that of 1850. Not surprisingly, more Guys were reported in London on Guy Fawkes Night 1850 than in recent memory.

In this new climate a movement grew to remove rather than to revive the service for 5 November, and with it the obsolete services for 30 January and 29 May. Some liberals found the seventeenth-century language 'offensive to the feelings of our catholic fellow subjects', or 'utterly repugnant to the religious feeling of the present day'. The institutionalized memory, they argued, was divisive and anachronistic. Hard-line conservatives, of course, disagreed. In Dublin, one zealous Protestant even tried to bring an action under the Act of Uniformity against a minister who omitted the special service for 5 November, but neither local magistrates nor the Queen's Bench in London would take up the case. As the archbishop of Canterbury observed in 1858, the service was 'irregularly disregarded' and had 'fallen into desuetude'.

During 1858 and 1859 the matter was before Parliament, and Lords and Commons debated the removal of the 'political' services that were still enshrined in statute. The speeches reported in Hansard reveal divided opinion on the value of remembering the Fifth of November, but general agreement that the time had come for change. George Hadfield, the Liberal member for Sheffield, found the ancient services 'offensive to every Christian', and was astonished that the statutes requiring them 'should have remained in existence for so many years'. Even the bishop of London acknowledged that the wording of the special prayers was 'likely to call up feelings of indignation in the breasts of their fellow countrymen'.

Leading the campaign for repeal, Lord Stanhope

did not for an instant deny that the deliverance of the sovereign and both houses of parliament from a sudden and cruel attack of conspirators was an act of providential mercy deserving to be held in grateful remembrance, and for which thanks were due to almighty God; nor was he inclined to speak in other terms than those of gratitude for the political and religious benefits which this country derived from the landing of King William III; but he submitted to their lordships that in all questions of this kind the lapse of time was a most important element. No man would think, for example, of celebrating by special thanks the expulsion of the Danes by King Alfred, or the return of Coeur de Lion from captivity.

The duke of Marlborough was reluctant to see change, and suggested that 'even if the services themselves were expunged, some memorial ought to be retained in the liturgy of the church of the events therein commemorated'. These events, he insisted,

were great events, calling for some solemn acknowledgement of gratitude, and [he told the Lords] he should be sorry to see the recollection of those events done away with in the future, and the matter passed over in silence. The particular mode of commemoration enjoined by the acts of parliament might possibly not be suited to the present day, but a mode might have been adopted which would have answered all the required purpose in duly testifying the national gratitude for these great events.

Finally, the Anniversary Days Observance Act became law in March 1859, and a tradition of two and a half centuries' duration came to a close. Observance of the Fifth of November was removed from the calendar of the established Church of England, to continue henceforth as an unofficial and secular tradition.

Much of the vitality of Gunpowder Treason Day from year to year came from its utility as a vehicle for dramatizing current political concerns. The street theatre of placards and processions, crowds and disguises, effigies and bonfires lent itself to the derisive depiction of political figures who had played no part in the original drama of the seventeenth century.

In 1745, after the Stuart rebellion, the fading anniversary of 5 November was revived by burning effigies of the Pope and the Pretender. In 1785 'the greasy rogues' of London 'dressed up a tall thin figure and . . . instead of "pray remember the fifth of

November", the cry was "pray remember Pitt and the shop tax"'. In 1788, it was reported, 'some arch dogs carried a Charles Fox' in the same manner as effigies of Guy Fawkes, 'and exalted him at the bonfire'. In 1792 it was the turn of the duke of Brunswick. The Revolution Society held its annual dinner on 5 November, with toasts to the French Revolution. The date was a popular dining night for Orange lodges. The anti-Catholic agitations of 1850 produced effigies of Pope Pius IX and the new cardinal archbishop of Westminster, along with 'St Guy the martyr'. The Crimean War years saw burning effigies of Tsar Nicholas on 5 November. Interest in Italian affairs in 1867 produced a pageant of the Pope about to be struck down by Garibaldi on Guy Fawkes Night. *The Times* reported: 'In many districts the ritualists shared with the pope the honour of being represented as "guys".'

Foreign and imperial affairs brought new figures into the Guy Fawkes pageant. Effigies of the 1870s included Pope Leo XIII, the Tsar of Russia, the Sultan of Turkey, the Amir of Afghanistan, Araby Pasha and the king of the Zulus. The Irish leader Parnell appeared on the bonfires in 1879. As *The Times* wryly noted in 1880, many of the 'guys . . . had nothing to do with the hero of the Gunpowder Plot, but rather burlesqued the incidents of the present time'. Historical memory gave way to current affairs.

The beginning of the twentieth century saw the burning of effigies of militant suffragists; and in 1909 the Hampstead bonfire featured a placard representing Lloyd George's Budget. Later it was the turn of the Kaiser and Adolf Hitler, among other celebrities, to go up in flames. And in the England of the 1980s and 1990s, Mrs Thatcher and some of her ministers have been similarly honoured, alongside diabolized Third World bogey men like Saddam Hussein.

From the eighteenth century to the present, local animosities

often substituted an unpopular neighbour for the figure of the Guy. The Somerset diarist James Woodforde recorded on 5 November 1768 that 'the effigy of Justice Creed was had through the streets of Castle Cary this evening upon the [fire] engine, and then had into the park and burnt in a bonfire immediately before the Justice's house . . . the whole parish are against the Justice.' Victorian worthies who were similarly burned in effigy included local Members of Parliament, an enemy of the Kettering shoemakers, four 'persons prominent in the Plumstead common agitation', and the disgraced borough councillors of St Albans who had illegally enclosed land in Sandpit Lane.

The riotousness of Guy Fawkes Night, especially notorious in the late eighteenth and early nineteenth centuries, diminished from the mid-Victorian period as public officials determined to bring the festivities under control. The sale of fireworks was regulated and in some places prohibited. Police and magistrates planned strategies to avoid the worst excesses, contesting with revellers for control of the streets. In 1847 the authorities at Lewes determined to restrain the annual disorder, and brought in extra detachments of police and troops. The result was a series of skirmishes between 'bonfire boys' and the constabulary, with some of the tradesmen taking the revellers' side and others barricading their doors. The authorities at Guildford similarly reinforced themselves in 1863 with 160 special constables, 50 dragoons, 150 soldiers and two local corps of rifle volunteers in reserve. 'Several bands of roughs' disputed this show of force, but the mayor read the Riot Act (although there was no riot), and constables with drawn truncheons attempted to clear the streets.

Within a few years this policy of intervention paid off; respectability and decorum began to prevail in this area of Victorian life as in so many others. At Godalming in 1870, *The*

Times reported, 'the preparations made for the preservation of order were enough to overawe the most determined peace-breakers.' Guildford and Lewes, formerly famous for their extravagance on Guy Fawkes Night, saw the anniversary pass without incident. At Oxford and Cambridge, where Gunpowder Night violence once pitted town against gown, the proctors and constables worked to prevent serious disturbances. By 1876 it could be claimed that 'the utmost decorum prevailed' at Oxford, and the following year 'the anniversary of the Gunpowder Plot passed off very tamely in the metropolis.' Guy Fawkes Night had been tamed.

Further changes took place in the late nineteenth century, as the anarchic elements of Guy Fawkes Night gave way to organized entertainment. The middle class returned to the cere-mony, and took over. Bonfires and street activities which had once been the work of 'roughs' and 'idle mobs' now became the planned projects of societies and clubs. Special committees sprang up throughout southern England to mount and to man-age the Guy Fawkes celebrations. The 'principal inhabitants' who had earlier withdrawn behind their shutters on 5 November now came forth as proud sponsors. Landowners provided special fields for the bonfires, thereby diverting the most danger-ous festivity from the centres of towns. The more menacing aspects of the Guy Fawkes tradition were eliminated, and a spectacle that had once been divisive and dangerous was remade in wholesome and benevolent garb. In several towns the aggressive masking and disguising of an earlier generation was channelled into jolly costume parades.

The Hitchin Bonfire Club organized torchlit parades in which more than 400 masqueraders took part. Dorchester enjoyed a procession of costumed 'guys', with music from the town band and a display of fireworks costing £50 – in 1879 the subscribers included Lord Alington and the local MP. At Horsham in 1880

the festivities took place 'with the sanction of the Local Board authorities, and under the patronage of most of the chief families of the town and district'. Bridgwater adopted 5 November for an elaborate annual carnival. Patriotic processions featured imperial themes. At Winchester the parade was headed by the city fire brigade, while at Salisbury the bonfire was lit by the mayor.

Previously scattered activities in London coalesced around the organized parades of the Lewisham Bonfire Society in the south and the Hampstead Bonfire Club in the north. Like their counterpart at Hitchin, these were social and philanthropic associations, reminiscent of medieval confraternities. A 'novelty' in 1880, the 'annual carnival' at Lewisham quickly became an established tradition. The procession featured bands, fancy dress, the banners of friendly societies and a smiling police escort, but it no longer concluded with a bonfire. On the other side of London the 'cavalcade' of the Hampstead Bonfire Society drew some 50,000 spectators to see costumed equestrians, musicians, a representation of Britannia and a grand bonfire on the heath. But the bonfire did not necessarily burn a Guy. By the Edwardian era this carnival had become a fund-raising event with 'Ye Olde Hampstead Bonfire Club' (the self-conscious archaism a sure sign of an invented tradition) collecting money for local hospitals.

The anniversary changed again in the twentieth century, with the triumph of the consumer society. Guy Fawkes Night became 'Firework Night' as commercial manufacturers like Brock or Paine stepped up production. The Brock company sold 30 million fireworks in 1908: Paine unloaded almost 500 tons. In 1909 a special set piece was available featuring *Dreadnought*, a model of the great battleship which 'explodes with a fiery display'. *The Times* observed that year that 'firework parties are becoming quite an institution in the suburban districts'. In 1910 the demand for fireworks was said to be up 25–30 per cent from the previous year. Firework enthusiasm was set aside during the Great War, but resumed in the 1920s, when much of the money-raising activity of children – 'a penny for the Guy' – was intended to purchase fireworks. The festivity became increasingly the concern of children – more an amusement than a commemoration – so that a correspondent in 1930 suggested turning the Fifth of November into 'Children's play day'. Children's firework parties, with adult supervision, became a common feature of childhood memories of the 1950s and 1960s. The instruction 'light the blue touch paper and retire immediately' still evokes a kaleidoscope of sounds, lights and smells.

The early twenty-first century has seen further modifications to the tradition, mostly in the direction of safety and control. Fewer children handle fireworks or build bonfires; more attend spectacles put on by charitable or service organizations. With paid admission, spectator areas and a narrated programme, the fireworks 'show' has increasingly replaced the bonfire party. The rockets go higher and burst with more colour, but they have less and less to do with memories of the Fifth of November. The story of Gunpowder Treason, once taught from the pulpit and revenged in the streets, is now a history lesson in schools. Furthermore, the expensive displays of fireworks put on to celebrate royal and patriotic occasions have in recent years stolen the thunder of the Fifth of November. It might be observed that Guy Fawkes Night is finally declining, having lost its connection with politics and religion. But we have heard that many times before.

From being a matter of life and death that threatened 'the

martyrdom of the kingdom' the Gunpowder Plot had been transformed into (*The Times*'s phrase) 'an annual jest'. Over 400 years it has been associated with a creative festive tradition, with shifting sponsorship, varying intensity and periodic re-infusions of meaning. As a late Stuart almanac put it, 'what ere's forgot, the memory of the Powder Plot will hardly die'. Shaped and reshaped by social, religious and political currents, the anniversary of the Fifth of November has proved remarkably hardy and remarkably versatile. It has endured as a cultural phenomenon because of its mutability, because English society has repeatedly reinfused it with fresh meanings.

It appears, then, that the long history of the Fifth of November is not one of simple survival or customary continuity, but rather one of recurrent reconstruction, remaking and adaptation to changing concerns. The calendar provided the grid, the anniversary supplied the occasion, but its meaning, its social location and its religious, political and cultural implications have repeatedly been subject to change. Even now, we remember, remember. But part of the task of history is to keep memory honest.

One final custom deserves mention. The practice of searching the cellars at Westminster, re-enacting the vigilance that discovered Guy Fawkes in 1605, is believed to date from the 1690s when a second Gunpowder Plot was feared. This custom has continued as a quaint anachronism, a parliamentary folly, involving lamplit searches (ignoring the electricity), and concluding with cakes and wine for the Beefeaters. In 1812 *The Times* reported the ritual searching of the cellars at Westminster before the opening of Parliament. The Lord High Chamberlain, the Usher of the Black Rod, a Yeoman Usher and a dozen Yeomen of the Guard conducted their search, 'according to custom, since the days of Guy Faux'. The last cellar they came to was occupied by a wine-merchant, so 'some of the inspectors tasted the contents of the pipes, to ascertain that they did not contain gunpowder.'

CHAPTER FOUR

Popes and Guys and Anti-Catholicism

JUSTIN CHAMPION

> Charm! Song! And Show! A murder and a Ghost!
> We know not what you desire or hope
> To please you more, but burning of a Pope.
>
> *John Dryden*

Bonfire Night is a despicable relic of a culture that commended, in the name of Christian duty, the persecution of religious minorities, the burning of witches and the ritual desecration of suicides. Its persistence in modern culture is unacceptable: that such a supposedly festive ritual, celebrating the immolation of an individual, has been exploited as a political device which stigmatizes a religious minority within the broader community makes it even more obscene. The fact that each year a number of children suffer accidental mutilation, and sometimes even death, through innocently participating in such a gruesome event is still bewildering to many. The tenacity of the ritual in the twenty-first century is a relic of an earlier and more brutal age. Far from commemorating the escape of the Protestant political elite from destruction, to many (even today) it is a residual act of anti-Catholic hatred that still reveals the essentially Protestant foundations of modern political culture in the United Kingdom. Protestant communities in Northern Ireland have successfully reinvented and invigorated festive, and not so festive, displays of historical memory with the marching season and the communal activities remembering the godly defiance of the apprentice boys at the siege of Derry. Few within the broader public on the 'mainland' would recognize or acknowledge that, from the perspective of the Roman Catholic minority in England, Bonfire Night may have had as much oppressive force as much of the semi-militaristic display of the Orange marching bands. Recovering the reactions of Roman Catholic minorities to public memorials like Bonfire Night has rarely been attempted.

Even today it is not uncommon for many to remember Guy Fawkes Night not as a moment of collective celebration but as one of exclusion. When parents refuse invitations to Guy Fawkes parties – they may be overly sensitive to cultural traditions, but the seven or eight year old, unaware of the burdens of memory, is acutely conscious of the feeling of being excluded from the fun. Neighbours caution certain families of the potential 'difficulties' of their presence. The mimicry of burning a condemned criminal is itself a vicious act, another remnant of the brutality of the pre-modern state – but an act liable to spill over into more contemporary combustion.

At a time when liberal sensitivities are rightly outraged at the inhumane treatment meted out in the name of 'freedom' at Guantánamo Bay, it is worth recalling the routine nature of dismemberment and butchery fundamental to the display of state power in the seventeenth and eighteenth centuries. It might also be remembered that Irish Roman Catholic communities both in Ireland and on the 'mainland' have borne the brunt of paramilitary and judicial punishment. While it is difficult to estimate the total number of Roman Catholics who suffered persecution and death across the period, there are glimpses of the cruelty in moments of political and military crisis. Hundreds of priests were executed, thousands of families were reduced to penury and poverty through fines and imprisonment. The

most brutal atrocities are associated with the wars in Ireland in the 1640s and the early 1690s. One contemporary, the statistician William Petty, writing in the 1670s, estimated that over half a million Catholics (about 41 per cent of the entire Irish population) perished one way or another in the military conflict in Ireland in the 1640s and 1650s. Malnutrition, battle, siege, assassination and state execution were routine means of dispatch.

This treatment, which could be regarded as ethnic cleansing, was perpetuated in the eighteenth century: as late as 1798, in quelling the Irish rebellion, it was reported that 30,000 civilians were killed. The Protestant mind of the period regarded such atrocity as God's work: the extermination of Irish papists was a providential duty – it was striking at the forces of Antichrist. Some of the more extreme 'hot' Protestant views can be seen in Oliver Cromwell's declaration in 1650 to the Catholic clergy: 'you are part of Antichrist, whose Kingdom the Scriptures so expressly speaks should be laid in blood ... and ere it be long, you must all of you have blood to drink'. The massacres at Drogheda and Wexford, for example, were explicitly celebrated as 'just judgements and righteous justice'. Many, in England, have forgotten these terrors. But just as the papacy in 1970 was still conferring sainthood on Catholic victims of the Popish Plot, so Catholic cultural memory is sensitized to the significance of Bonfire Night. Despite achieving a measure of emancipation in the nineteenth century, the experience of Catholics, especially Irish Catholics, into the twentieth and twenty-first centuries has not been a happy one. By placing the memory of such atrocity so prominently in our mind's eye it may be possible to recognize that Guy Fawkes's end is a strange and violent act to remember. In our modern pluralist age we are encouraged to exercise tolerance towards other faiths and religious rituals; there are, however, moments when the bare bones of earlier ages puncture the fabric of modernity – Bonfire Night is one of those moments.

For many Roman Catholics, even today, Bonfire Night prompts painful collective memories of persecution, punishment and martyrdom. As good citizens today merrily set fire to effigies of Guy Fawkes, they might usefully pause to consider the suffering and pain which Catholic communities in England, Scotland and Ireland have experienced over the course of the last four centuries. English Protestant society was a persecuting culture. The threat of Catholic subversion or military invasion in the Elizabethan period had seen the development of legislation which subjected Roman Catholics to penalties and punishments for practising their faith, for not conforming to the doctrine and liturgy of the established Church and for refusing to take oaths of political loyalty to the sovereign. After the Pope had excommunicated Elizabeth I in 1570, Roman Catholics by default became political subversives, since the thrust of the Papal Bull was to declare Elizabeth a heretic: as every good Catholic understood, it was not possible to obey, or keep faithful promises, with such a heretic. Fines, deprivations, imprisonment and executions were the instruments of anti-Catholic policy.

Loyal Roman Catholics were in a classic bind – their religious conscience insisted upon conformity to the counsel of the Pope; their political loyalty may have been to their sovereign. Obeying two authorities was impossible: while some English Catholics developed a brand of moral casuistry (the most obvious remnant of this today is the practice of crossing one's fingers when being less than straightforward with the truth) that allowed them to conform publicly while maintaining religious integrity in the privacy of the domestic sphere. The so-called anti-recusancy penal laws (those who refused to take the Anglican communion or to swear oaths of obligation were known as recusants) aimed to bring Catholic priests and lay people to a conformity: those who refused were deprived of their civil rights, their property, and ultimately their lives.

Statutes of Supremacy and Uniformity, passed and revised during the Elizabethan settlement, laid the foundations for subsequent treatment of every Catholic dissident in the seventeenth century. Acknowledging the spiritual authority of the Pope became a crime punished by confiscation, fine and imprisonment. Serial offenders were liable to the charge of high treason: punishment in this case was hanging, drawing and quartering. The families of such criminals were also punished: heirs were incapable of inheriting honours and offices; all property was forfeited to the Crown. Any who refused oaths of loyalty to the Crown were subjected to the same penalties. At a more routine level, the Act of Uniformity was concerned with religious conformity: clergymen and lay people were fined ($12d.$) each time they missed church services. These sorts of fine cumulatively destroyed the economic welfare of individual families and impoverished the Catholic community. The great diaspora of Irish Catholics to the New World was not the product of adventure and opportunity, but of brutal persecution.

After the excommunication of the queen, the most severe statutes tightened up the punishments for those who were disloyal: it was high treason for anyone to be 'reconciled' to Catholicism. Again, potentially massive fines, lengthy imprisonment and possible death might be imposed for repeated worship at Catholic Masses. The fine for not attending Anglican service was raised to £20 a month – a huge sum in today's terms (an average income for a farmer might be £30–£40 a year!). Some Acts specifically stigmatized clergymen and seminary priests: the Jesuits were particularly singled out as the most insidious group, and consequently suffered martyrdom in large numbers. According to some accounts, more than 150 Catholics died on

the scaffold between 1581 and 1603. As we shall see, these numbers are a fraction of those who died in the following century.

The thrust of the many anti-popish laws during the period before and after the Plot was to define Catholics as 'rebellious and traitorous subjects'. This legislative culture provided the immediate context for the anxieties and brutality that the Gunpowder Plot provoked. James I, far from offering tenderness to Catholics, explicitly endorsed and reinforced earlier laws: new oaths of allegiance and associated statutes imposed ever heavier fines, confiscations, longer imprisonments and cruel punishments. Catholic communities were subject to discipline in their lives, religion and property: they were banned from all forms of public service (so they could not legally be lawyers or doctors, hold civil offices, or act in any military capacity). New Acts along similar lines were passed in the 1670s and after 1689. The threat of Catholic support for the deposed Stuart monarchy in the form of a Jacobite invasion meant that even in the eighteenth century penalties were increased. For example, the most routine form of discrimination was the imposition of land tax at double rate. Imagine the government today insisting that all Muslims must pay twice the rate of income tax.

These legal instruments provided a complete means for discrimination against the Catholic community. While it is clear that enforcement in England, Scotland and Ireland across the period was sporadic and regional – times of political crisis were the usual prompt for fierce implementation, as we shall see – it is also clear that many of these laws persisted on the statute books into the nineteenth century. In the case of Ireland, it should also be remembered that there was an intensification of persecution after 1689: the triumph of 'King Billy' empowered the Protestant ascendancy to attempt to destroy the Catholic faith by measures of forced conversion. The constitutional legislation forbidding Catholic accession to the throne is still established law.

Given the increasing public sensitivity about criticism and hostility towards other people's religious belief, it is surprising that Bonfire Night still persists as a supposedly collective moment of cultural commemoration. Remnants of the once dominant anti-Catholic prejudices of the establishment are still evident when a new Minister of State for Education is 'exposed' as a member of a Roman Catholic secret society. Catholics in public politics are still fair game, where Jews and Muslims are not. Treatment of 'other' religions is increasingly sensitive in the public media: the case of Roman Catholicism still seems to be a legitimate target. The constitutional insistence that a British monarch should not be allowed to marry a Catholic is a powerful vestige of the Protestant foundations of our modern political culture – Bonfire Night is a powerful moment for subliminally confirming these prejudices.

Contrary to popular belief, effigies of Guy Fawkes only started to be burned on bonfires in the eighteenth century. Traditionally, on seventeenth-century bonfires it was elaborate models of the Pope and his co-conspirators that were designed for destruction. Sometimes such effigies were paraded around the streets and pelted with mud and ordure; at other times cats were trapped – their howls of pain meant to signify the wailing of the Whore of Babylon. Contemporary prints of some of the events certainly suggest a very sophisticated ritual – contemporaries describe models of the Pope processing to the great bonfire accompanied by Jesuitical plotters and devils: there were 'mighty bonfires and ye burning of a most costly pope, caryed by four persons in divers habits, and ye effigies of 2 divells whispering in his eares, his belly filled full of live catts who squawled most hideously'.

Contemporary engravings displayed the pageant of satire

against the Catholic faith and a prediction of future plots against Protestantism – the *processio Romana* included priests, friars, bishops, cardinals armed to the teeth. As the verses on the Jesuit float noted, 'It is our faith, our principle, our trade/ Through purple floods of Monarch's blood to wade/To burn, destroy, confound, Assassin kill/A Jesuit can do nothing but what's ill'. Such public burnings, sometimes accompanied by the destruction of confiscated Catholic property (relics, vestments, prayer books), were enormously popular – it is estimated that at one such burning in 1679 more than 200,000 watched the pyre at Temple Bar in London. While it is difficult to recover the experience of repression the Roman Catholic minorities suffered, their victimhood was publicly manifest in the executions, lynchings, imprisonment, fines and political exclusion they experienced into the nineteenth century. Evident too is the powerful political instrument the repression of 'popery' delivered into the hands of those who held the reins of national government.

The image of the popish plotter dominated both print and visual culture in the seventeenth and eighteenth centuries. A work which combines both media, *The Protestants Vade Mecum, or Popery Display'd in its proper colours, in Thirty Emblems, lively representing all the Jesuitical Plots against this nation* (1680), takes great care to present a persuasive and illustrated narrative of the 'hellish designe' of popery against the true religion, each image confirmed with an appropriate scriptural reference. Starting with an emblem of Jesuits plotting against Henry VIII, the book describes the history of the sixteenth and seventeenth centuries as punctuated by popish plots – the persecution of Bloody Mary, the Armada conspiracy, the Gunpowder Plot (neatly illustrated with an extract from Job (24:16): 'In the dark they dig through houses, which they had marked for themselves in the daytime; they know not the light'),

the murder of Charles I, the burning of London, are all linked in a crescendo of conspiracy. The last seventeen emblems deliver a detailed narrative of the ongoing Popish Plot exposed by Titus Oates. Visual narratives of plots were also produced in other forms – playing cards exposed the main players and vilified the guilty: the Gunpowder Plot and the Popish Plot of 1678 both inspired the equivalent of strip cartoons to show the reality of the conspiracies. These all fomented a politics of fear: Protestant communities were anxious that popish atrocity was imminent; Roman Catholics were the constant target of public discipline and exclusion.

The identification of Roman Catholics, more specifically Jesuits, as a persisting and devious fifth column ever ready to destroy true religion was also a staple element in many of the political engravings of the period. In one of the most controversial pieces – 'A project of a Popish successor displayed by hell bred cruelty, popish villainy, strange divinity, intended slavery, old English misery' – the central figure is half-Irish Catholic, half-devil (complete with cloven hoof and horned head). With one hand the figure (trampling with one foot on skulls, with the other on the crown) sets light to faggots that will burn Protestant martyrs, while a sanctified trumpet blows flames that kindle fires in London and Westminster. In the background, clergymen, under the whip of another horned and winged devil, drive the Church towards Rome.

The continuity of these images of Jesuitical conspirators, inspired by devils, aiming to overturn the Protestant state can be seen in the powerful engraving prepared for Oliver Cromwell (in the late 1650s) and adapted for the reign of William III in the 1690s. The 'Embleme of Englands Distraction' represents the figures of Cromwell and William bringing freedom and happiness to England; the two pillars of Church and state support a godly community, with the eye of providence, the dove of peace and the angel of fame looking benignly on. In the background, a divine wind steers the ship of state between Scylla and Charybdis. Both figures trample underfoot the Whore of Babylon and the many-headed Hydra of error. In the bottom-right-hand corner, hidden from the view of the ploughmen and agricultural labourers, papists set about undermining the foundations of the pillars of the state with pickaxes, while another applies the bellows to the lighted fuse leading to barrels of gunpowder – in the foreground, Jesuits sanctify these conspiratorial actions. These images of plotters, arsonists and assassins haunted the political landscape of seventeenth- and eighteenth-century society.

The legacy of the Gunpowder Plot shaped popular and elite attitudes to political and religious crisis. The fear of real, and imagined, Roman Catholics, even if they were a minority, was rendered more dangerous by perceptions of international con-spiracy. Whether they were colluding with the Spanish, French or Irish, the memory of the Gunpowder Plot delivered a template for understanding subsequent political crisis. The fear of popery became a cultural force capable of being mobilized not simply by the government, but even sometimes against the government.

Writing in 1679, the radical pamphleteer Charles Blount described the bloody spectacle he insisted it had been, 'the last time Popery reigned amongst us':

First, imagine you see the whole town in flames . . . at the same instant, fancy amongst the distracted crowd you behold troops of Papists ravishing your wives and daughters, dashing your little children's brains out against the walls, plundering your houses and cutting your own throats . . . Then represent to yourselves the Tower of London playing off its cannon, and battering down your houses about your ears. Also, casting your eye towards Smithfield, imagine you see your

Though Hell, Rome, and France: have United their Powers: We Defie them all Three (Sir)

father, or your mother, or some of your nearest and dearest relations, tied to a stake in the midst of flames, when with hands and eyes lifted up to heaven, they cry out to God for whose cause they die.

Seventeenth-century English, Irish, Welsh and Scottish men, women and children lived their lives in the perpetual fear that the next Popish Plot would be successful: the eternal vigilance of the watchful, aided by providential protection, was all that saved the godly city from the 'black crew of papists'. The dark plot inspired by the wiles of the Roman Antichrist was potentially to manifest itself in assassination, treason, arson, rape and massacre. There was, as the single-page broadside *The pedigree of Popery; or the genealogie of antichrist* (1688) asserted, a historical and logical connection between the devil and the rule of popery – carnal policy and the mystery of iniquity had created the Jesuits, who had in turn inspired the monsters of 'Atheism, tyranny, treason, assassination, perjury, inquisition, massacre, masquerade and open popery, City burning . . .', the list goes on and on before concluding: 'and all kinds of abominations, which walking abroad in a dress of religion and dissimulation, complete the whole train of Antichrist'. The evidence of the Gunpowder Plot was a providentially exposed tip of a much deeper and perdurable conspiracy: seventeenth-century Protestants were convinced that behind every political difficulty or religious corruption lay 'popish' subterfuge.

The vision of the triumph of popery laid a political foundation for stigmatizing any oppositional milieu. Anti-popery, inspired by the revelation of the near-miss of 1605, provided propaganda which dwarfs the effectiveness of the anti-communist scares of McCarthyite America, or even the 'war on terrorism' today. Anxiously conjuring up powerful images of the downfall of Protestant civilization consequent on the restoration of Roman Catholicism, Blount went on to describe how 'Beautiful

Churches, erected for the true worship of God' would be 'abused and turned into idolatrous temples, to the dishonour of Christ, [and] scandal of religion'. 'Our apparent ruin stands at hand,' he lamented, 'the sword already hangs over our heads, and seems to be supported by no stronger force than that of a single hair, his Majesty's life.' If anything should happen to Charles II, 'let no other noise be heard among you but that of arm, arm to revenge your sovereign's death.'

Blount's short pamphlet was a powerful call to arms – it invoked every anti-Catholic stereotype to provoke a visceral and violent fear among the Protestant communities of England of the clear and present danger of popish sedition. Charles Blount's tocsin of alarm was sounded against the fear of a Popish Plot to assassinate Charles II. The foundations of that political fear, mobilized against James, duke of York, were laid in the events and political capital generated by the discovery of the Gunpowder Plot in 1605. It is no exaggeration to claim that these gut fears and prejudices determined and defined the great political crises of the seventeenth century from the outbreak of Civil War in the 1640s, to the Exclusion crisis of the early 1680s, to the final triumph of the Protestant state after 1689.

The influence of the events of 5 November 1605 resonated down the succeeding decades. Like tiny embers, at times the power of the cultural memory of plot, conspiracy and papal threat may have lain dormant in the storehouse of the country, but it only took the mildest political crisis to encourage the fiercest flames back to life as the episode of the Popish Plot and the consequent crisis of monarchical succession demonstrates. A very rough count of printed works produced across the seventeenth century that vilified 'popery' shows that about 800 were produced: the great peaks of publication were, unsurprisingly, at times of the most profound political crisis – the early 1640s, the late 1670s and 1689 saw hundreds of titles in circulation, feeding public anxieties. Anti-popery was the ingredient that consistently radicalized and destabilized already difficult political situations.

The first significant political crisis shaped by the legacy of anti-Catholic prejudice ended with the monarch on the scaffold. During the 1630s Charles I's increasingly autocratic style of government, coupled with the religious policy of Archbishop Laud, had led many to regard his regime as tainted by popish inclination. The so-called Bishops' War saw military conflict between a Scottish army hostile to religious innovation, and a king determined to confirm his authority. By August 1640 the Scots had invaded and defeated Charles's forces at Newcastle; the negotiation of a truce at Ripon, the terms a postponement of final settlement until Parliament was called and royal payment of all military expenses (the massive sum of £850 a day), ensured that a new Parliament was inevitable.

The new Parliament intended to punish the instigators of Charles I's personal rule: evil advisers rather than the king himself were the focus of hostilities. Members of Parliament hoped to re-establish the traditional harmony of king and people by purging the body politic of corrupt and evil counsellors. Popery had contaminated the court but not the king. These political anxieties were directed against the king's closest advisers – Thomas Wentworth (created Lord Strafford in 1640 for services to the court), architect of regal policy in Ireland and England, and Archbishop Laud, inspiration behind the anti-Puritan ecclesiastical regime. On 24 November 1640 Strafford's impeachment began. In March 1641 Laud was formally charged with attempting to reconcile England to Rome. Strafford was indicted with attempting to alter the fundamental laws of England and treasonably encouraging Catholic designs against England.

The fall of Strafford is an epitome of the power that the fear of popery had to poison the relationship between king, Parliament and people. Charles was loath to lose his minister, and he was prepared to turn to any source, even foreign Catholics, to strike back at the rebellious Scots. In the Commons, John Pym, the outspoken critic of royal policy in the 1620s, was determined to expose the Catholic conspiracy that threatened England. On 3 May 1641 Pym announced news of an Army Plot, hatched to spring Strafford from the Tower. London was reduced to fearful panic. In response, the Commons drew up an oath of allegiance whereby MPs, and ultimately the whole population, would swear an oath in defence of the 'true reformed Protestant religion', the king and Parliament and 'the lawful rights and liberties of the subject'. By default, Roman Catholics were regarded as seditious conspirators.

That the fear of a popish conspiracy gained popular currency at this time is indisputable. This panic converted itself into extra-parliamentary agitation and popular demonstration; fear was to drive the political crisis to a bloody end. More than 20,000 Londoners had petitioned for Strafford's death. In the first week of May huge gatherings of 'mechanic people' had mobbed the House of Lords and Whitehall demanding that Charles sign the death warrant, which he duly did (with much regret) on 10 May. Strafford was executed two days later. At the same time Charles signed an Act of Parliament that ensured Parliament could not be dissolved without its own consent. The pattern of constitutional reform against the practices of the personal rule being driven by an ever-increasing parliamentary and popular hysteria about the existence of a Catholic conspiracy against Protestantism was to be repeated over and over again during the 1640s. Ultimately this spiral of hostility against a Popish Plot tainted Charles I himself.

The fear of popish conspiracy was orchestrated by John Pym

in the Commons but directed to a national audience in the provinces. It was Pym's firm belief, and one that he had held since the rise of Laudianism in the 1620s, that a Catholic conspiracy surrounded Charles I and threatened Protestant liberties. Evil counsellors perverted royal policy; Jesuit advisers haunted Whitehall; Catholic soldiers prepared for a coup. Pym aimed to root out this conspiracy and erect political and military bulwarks against its resurgence. Political and religious reforms passed through Parliament unpicking corrupted institutions and practices. Star Chamber and the other prerogative courts used by Laud and Strafford in the 1630s against the godly were abolished. Ship money, knighthood fines, purveyances and forest laws were all removed. Earlier a Triennial Act had been passed, determining that a Parliament had to be called every three years.

Fundamental to Pym's strategy of settlement between king and Parliament was the series of *Ten Propositions* put forward in June 1641. These plans consisted of purging evil counsellors, rooting out popery and defending the realm against internal and external invasion. The Commons would assume control of those who advised the king. There would be strict enforcement of the recusancy laws against Catholics. The militia and ports were to be 'made fit for service' against potential conspirators. The spectre of a papist plot was to be foiled.

Pym's strategy to force a reformed settlement reached a high point in the early days of November 1641. Pym and his fellow committeemen had been working on a much longer proposal for reform since August. Based on the *Ten Propositions*, the *Grand Remonstrance*, which was addressed as much to the people as to the king, set out in precise detail the history of popish conspiracy since the 1620s and the proposed remedies. The king's foreign, financial and religious policies were indicted: a catalogue of fifteen years of 'evils and corruptions' was condemned. The *Remonstrance* continued to uphold Parliament as the legitimate source of such remedies and settlement with the king. Dramatically, before the document could be introduced into the Commons, revelations of the Irish rebellion reached the House on 1 November. This set the scene for the final breakdown of relations between king and Parliament. The power of Pym's reforms had been given credibility by the fear of Catholic conspiracy – his management of revelations of Army Plots and attempts on true Protestants provided justification for such policies.

The news of a real rebellion, complete with tales of atrocious murders and massacres of godly Protestants by Irish Catholics, gave substance to the conspiracies Pym had uncovered. Rumours of similar attempts in England and the Irish rebels' profession of loyalty to Charles set the final seeds of distrust between king and Parliament. It is difficult now to capture the atmosphere of these days, but there was a real and profound fear of murder and massacre throughout the country and particularly in London.

Richard Baxter's reaction to the news of the Irish rebellion in autumn 1641 summarizes Protestant feelings: 'it filled all England with a fear both of the Irish and the Papist at home . . . insomuch that when the rumour of a plot was occasioned at London, the poor people, all the counties over, were ready either to run to arms, or hide themselves, thinking that the Papist were ready to rise and cut their throats.' News of the massacre of perhaps as many as 12,000 true English Protestants by the bloodthirsty papists acted as a massive stimulant to popular political fears of a Catholic conspiracy against true religion in England. Pym's speculations were proving to be accurate. Foreign Catholics, evil advisers, Cavaliers and Royalist delinquents became lumped together in the popular mind. People put chains across the streets to warn them of armed troops.

Rumours of strangers, Irishmen and Jesuits, spread from county to county and town to town. Spontaneous attacks upon Catholics, and suspected conspirators, added to the hysteria. Thomas Beale gave evidence that two men in collusion with Catholic priests had organized 108 men to assassinate a similar number of 'puritan' peers and MPs as a signal for a general rising.

In the shadows cast by the Rebellion, the light of the *Remonstrance* looked even more brilliant. Leading Catholics were imprisoned and Parliament took control of the militia. The *Remonstrance* was passed by eleven votes in the Commons, and was printed and distributed around the kingdom. It was from this point that MPs and Lords began to form into Royalist and anti-Royalist groups. Ultimately, these interests fought for their beliefs on the battlefields of England, Scotland and Ireland. The fear of popery had determined the growth of mutual distrust between king, Parliament and people. The dual fears of political tyranny and religious corruption became entangled. The worries of a plot or conspiracy against Protestant liberties had turned into a political reality by 1642.

The popular dimensions of fear and hysteria about such a plot, made more diffuse by the massive explosion of printed newsletters and broadsides spreading rumours and tales, were a crucial determinant on the road to the Civil War. For a war to be fought two sides had to be mobilized: foot-soldiers were needed as well as generals. The evidence of the localities' interest and close attention to developments at Westminster and the Palace of Whitehall is manifest in the numerous petitions and demonstrations for and against the plot. This politicization of the people itself led to the polarization of the nation in the summer of 1642. Some pointed to the clear evidence of a popish conspiracy to overthrow true religion and decided to arm themselves against bishops and princes, while others, gesturing at the burgeoning outbreaks of disorder and riot, suggested that the greater threat was that of social disintegration and mobilized behind the keystone of order – the king – against the Puritan rebels.

During the English revolution of the 1640s and 1650s, while the generalized fear of popery acted as a white noise of political discourse, the challenge of sectarianism and popular political radicalism preoccupied both provincial communities and national magistrates. Under the helm of the Lord Protector, Oliver Cromwell, providence briefly enabled the elect nation to pursue godly reformation: this godly project disintegrated into military chaos and prophetic conflict in the late 1650s after Cromwell's untimely death. Remarkably, many of the popular pamphlets of the period still employed the vocabulary of popish conspiracy to stigmatize oppositional groups: one explanation for the efflorescence of religious sectarianism was that the Roman Antichrist was masquerading in Protestant form. So, for example, Quakers were often represented in political prints as secret Jesuits who were cunningly using disguise to attack true religion – a theme that was carried through to the end of the seventeenth century. At a more philosophical level, writers like Thomas Hobbes extended the category of 'popery' to include any independent religious authority that challenged the sovereignty of the civil state.

The restoration of regal and ecclesiastical authority in 1660 was heralded as a providential moment. Anglican order had survived the challenges of popish tyranny and sectarian sedition; Charles II re-established social order and the government of bishops imposed Protestant piety. The war against all forms of popish conspiracy was reinvigorated: again, the image of Britannia besieged was reinforced by a providential understanding of contemporary events like the Great Fire of London of

1666. The immediate perception was that plotting Roman Catholics (probably French) had deliberately torched London – discoveries of caches of daggers, arrests of firework-makers and reports of fireballs made of gunpowder and brimstone provoked panic among the urban population. Priests, recusants and visiting Frenchmen all became the focus of fear. Later engravings, like *A true and full narrative of those two never to be forgotten deliverances* (1671), made the explicit link with earlier threats – the Great Fire of London was simply the latest instalment of the project started with the Armada invasion and the Gunpowder Plot.

A combination of Charles II's pro-French foreign policy, a potential Catholic heir, the open manipulation of Parliament, and the rigorous prosecution of Protestant nonconformity meant that increasingly during the mid-1670s both the court and the government became tainted with 'popery and arbitrary government'. To many moderate Protestants the alliance of the king with a persecuting Anglicanism conjured up the popish spectre of the 1630s. The build-up of the standing army to a figure of about 30,000 in 1678 only encouraged the anti-popish fears of many in the Commons and the localities. Studies of the counties show how during the 1670s the pattern of politics moved from the consensus of the 1660s to a process of confrontation: by-elections became increasingly the focus of bitter contestation between those who represented the court and those who represented the Protestant country. Important Protestant anniversaries such as the Fifth of November were celebrated with mass demonstrations against 'popery' and burnings of papal effigies. Privy Councillors and ministers were attacked in the Commons as 'popishly affected'.

The fear of 'popery' was powerfully resurgent in the late 1670s. It is important to understand that the political worry about 'popery' was not just a simple dread of Roman Catholics but was a complicated mixture of anxiety about politics, religion and history. Studies of the Catholic community in Britain show that after the Restoration there were perhaps only 60,000 believers, confined mainly to the north of England: a sect perhaps no bigger than that of the Quakers. Studies of the enforcement of anti-Catholic laws show how many local communities were very lax in enacting the penalties against real Roman Catholics. For example, in theory some £5 million was due to the Exchequer in fines by 1670: precisely £147 15s. 7d. had been collected. Neighbours were reluctant to persecute a largely quiescent community. For most of the 1670s, although there was a perceptible increase in the number of Catholics prosecuted (the total income from fines increased to £78 5s. 6d. in 1675), real Catholics were not scapegoated. But as Bishop Samuel Parker commented, 'there were two inchanting terms, which at the first pronunciation could, like Circe's intoxicating cups, change men into beasts, namely, Popery and the French interest.'

This political terror, prompted by the fear of popery, was shaped by the aggressive military threat of the Catholic Louis XIV. Many of those who gathered in the London coffee houses or shadowy meeting houses also diagnosed a threat closer to home: it was not just the fear of Catholic invasion but a real apprehension that there was an enemy within. Famously, Andrew Marvell, the Republican poet and pamphleteer, published in 1677 a popular work, *An Account of the Growth of Popery and Arbitrary Government*, which, in a very similar form to the *Remonstrances* and *Propositions* of the early 1640s, condemned the corruption of the administration by popery. Works like Marvell's became a cornerstone of an oppositional group within Parliament and the localities: this opposition was not coordinated nor yet a political party but a collection of men who felt themselves bound in common cause to defend

Protestantism and their 'lives, liberties and estates'. Since both the king and the Church of England were in explicit cooperation to persecute Dissent and to corrupt Parliament, they were implicated, just as Laud had been in the 1640s, as agents of 'popery'.

It was in this charged political atmosphere that the events of 1678–81 came about – a crisis that erupted over the discovery in late autumn 1678 of a Catholic conspiracy to kill the king, which brought home the consequent danger of the Catholic James, duke of York, as the next legitimate successor. The episode of the so-called Popish Plot is clear evidence for the persistence of the fear of popery in this period. The real consternation that gripped the mind and actions of the nation between 1678 and 1681 was a potential repetition of the crisis of popery that carried England to civil war in the early 1640s – more importantly, Englishmen relived the earlier years fearful not only of the dangers of arbitrary power but also of the destruction of civil war.

News of a Catholic plot to kill Charles II was first rumoured in late summer 1678. The supposed plot – and it seems very likely that there was no Catholic conspiracy at all – was concocted and then revealed by two informers. The mastermind was Titus Oates, a man who had been both an Anglican and a Catholic priest. His sidekick was the near insane Israel Tonge. They claimed to have infiltrated a Jesuit plot to assassinate Charles and replace him with James, backed by French arms. They presented some forty-three articles of evidence that suggested that Sir George Wakeman, the queen's physician, was going to poison the king for £10,000. Both Charles and his Lord Treasurer and chief political manager, Thomas, earl of Danby, were doubtful of the accusation, but because of the political climate were forced to take Oates's and Tonge's fabrications seriously. Oates felt that in order to implicate James, duke of

York, even further, he should forge letters from the conspirators to the duke's confessor Bedinfield, which would be intercepted by Charles II's secret service. Such was the incompetence of the fabricators that unfortunately the letters reached Bedinfield, who immediately alerted both James and Charles.

On 4 September the Plot took a more public turn when Oates and Tonge swore on oath before Sir Edmund Berry Godfrey the truth of their discovery: by now the charge had expanded to eighty-one articles and implicated not only Jesuits, but Benedictines, Dominicans and many Catholic peers. In late September Oates and Tonge presented their evidence to the Privy Council: both men were masters at manipulating circumstantial details to paint a plausible account. The turning point came on the night of 12/13 October when Sir Edmund Berry Godfrey was murdered. The coroner's report put his death down to the 'papists' who had presumably murdered him in an attempt to cover up the Plot. This sparked off mass hysteria around the country similar to the days of November 1641 in the aftermath of the Irish rebellion. Sir Thomas Player expressed the fears of many when he commented that 'he did not know but the next morning they might all rise with their throats cut'. To this day the murderers of Sir Edmund have not been identified; conspiracy theories still abound.

Rumours of risings in Ireland, Scotland and Wales were rife. Some claimed that 20,000 Irish troopers had been dispatched to slaughter all Protestants. The Commons organized committees of investigation: on 1 November they helped to fuel the fears by giving the Plot official credence in both Houses (without any opposition at all). There was, as their resolution read, 'and still is, a damnable and hellish Plot, contrived and carried on by the Popish recusants, for the assassinating and murdering of the King, and for the subverting of the Government, and rooting out and destroying the Protestant religion'. The fact that a

Frenchman was discovered near to the Commons with stores of gunpowder underscored the threat (the fact that he was a legitimate firework-maker was ignored). Anti-Catholic measures were invoked. All Catholics were relieved of political office and banished five miles from London. There was a sharp increase in the prosecution of local Catholics. There were lynchings. Outspoken men were executed (one minor figure had, rather foolishly, while drunk, shouted out 'the King is a great heretic, I would kill him myself'). In the summer of 1679 some nineteen innocent priests were executed. Importantly, much of the original propaganda of the early 1640s describing the earlier popish conspiracies was reprinted. Popular newspapers like the *Weekly Advice* fed the lower orders with fresh revelations and anti-papal narratives.

The consequences of the Plot were not, however, restricted to popular hysteria and increased persecution of innocent papists: it sparked off a massive political crisis about the nature of monarchical government and the succession. As early as November 1678 both Houses pleaded with Charles to remove the duke 'from his person and counsels'. By March 1679 James was exiled from England at his brother's request. The next immediate casualty was the earl of Danby, implicated in secret dealings with Louis XIV. Danby was accused of not only collaborating with Louis but also trying to cover up the plot. In order to save his leading minister from impeachment (and also the consequent exposure of his own duplicity), Charles dissolved the Cavalier Parliament in January 1679. This dissolution ushered in two years of unprecedented political conflict focused on the business of electioneering for a new Parliament.

As the Plot became a political reality in the storm of anti-Catholic hysteria, the political nation turned upon James, and ultimately upon the prerogatives of the monarchy itself.

Electioneering for the new Parliament was furious and fundamental. Fear of Catholic conspiracy, of the standing army, of
Danby's management and of the often brutal persecution of
true Protestants became the central issue of the campaigns in
the localities. The new Parliament was purged of the Cavalier
interest (only about 30 out of the 500-odd MPs were Anglican
Royalists). All those who had been 'managed' by Danby were
rejected. Having impeached Danby, the first Exclusion Parliament set about resolving the problem of a Catholic successor.
In May 1679 they brought in a bill to exclude James from the
crown: if James persisted in promoting his claim to the throne,
'he shall be adjudged guilty of high treason, and shall suffer the
pains penalties and forfeitures as in cases of high treason'. If
James returned to England uninvited he was again to be charged
with treason: it was legitimate 'in case of resistance to fight, and
him . . . by force to subdue'.

Charles had tried to neutralize the Exclusionist platform
by proposing a series of limitations upon the succession of a
Catholic king: to preserve the Protestantism of the Church of
England all ecclesiastical offices and promotions would be without the king's remit; no papist was to be allowed to sit in either
House of Parliament; no papist was to hold any political office;
and lastly, all Lord Lieutenants and officers in the navy were
to be appointed by Parliament. Those opposed to James feared
that such arrangements could not bind a corrupt king, and
Charles II was forced to prorogue and dissolve Parliament
before the Bill of Exclusion was confirmed. From this moment
until the prorogation of the Oxford Parliament in 1681 England
faced its greatest crisis since the 1640s. Hopes that a more
moderate Parliament might come to a compromise over the
succession were dashed in October 1679 when the new MPs
displayed even more rabid anti-popery: Charles responded by
insisting that the recently elected Commons would not actually

be permitted to sit until October or November of the following year.

Meanwhile, those who opposed the succession of James (known as the Whig Party) set about appealing to the political nation: exploiting the fear of popery was to be one of their most powerful weapons. In London and the provinces massive petitioning campaigns were organized. The Exclusionists, men who followed the more radical Whigs like Shaftesbury and the Republican Algernon Sidney, turned to extra-parliamentary means to focus their attack upon James and the 'popery' of the Stuart court, just as Pym had in the early 1640s. Exclusionists explicitly appealed to the middling people. As well as organizing petitions against James and popery, public demonstrations and marches – massive displays of anti-Catholic feeling – were evident in the infamous Pope-burning processions, organized by groups like the radical Green Ribbon Club in London. Radical Whigs agitated among the apprentices of London.

Elections for local parish offices became the focus of political conflict, since Parliament had been prorogued. Against this background there were yet further revelations: at one point it was suggested that James actually intended to kill Charles himself. The Oxford Parliament was to be a turning point. The Whig mobilization of the people of London and the counties was considered by many Anglican gentry to be bringing England back to the days of popular agitation of the 1640s and the threat of a world turned upside down. Royalists and Anglicans, learning the lessons of the 1640s, did not allow the Whigs to dominate popular politics. Throughout 1679–81, as the Whigs organized petitions in favour of exclusion, Anglican Tories organized rival petitions that abhorred exclusion. Tory interests in London were equally as efficient as Whigs in organizing apprentices for their own anti-Exclusionist demonstrations: rival bonfires burnt effigies of 'Jack Presbyter', modelled upon the Puritan regicides rather than the Pope. For the Royalists, 'popery' was at the root of these Whig plots. After the Oxford Parliament was dissolved, Charles and his bishops painted the agitators and their leaders – Shaftesbury, Russell and Sidney – as revolutionaries inspired by the papal Antichrist. There was a popery of the left and of the right.

As James, duke of York, commented, 'all the world sees that it is not religion that they drive at so much as the destruction of the monarchy'. By June 1683 the court had sufficient grounds to publicize evidence of a Whig plot to assassinate the king in the form of the Rye House Plot. Contemporary political engravings made this connection between dissenting plotting and Roman Catholic conspiracy very explicit. Even though it seems counter-intuitive to us today, there had long been an assertion that religious dissenters – Presbyterians, Baptists, Quakers and Ranters – were really Jesuits in disguise. Popery was subtle and shape-shifting: one of the most powerful representations, 'The Committee or Popery in Masquerade', presented the cabal between 'Little Isaac' and the 'Pope' to create misrule and irreligion. Images of monarchy and episcopacy were cast to the floor – Magna Charta and the Bible were discarded – while Anabaptists bearing daggers covenanted to restore popery: as the text explained, it was a 'motley schism; Half Pope, Half Puritan; who whilst they talk of Union, Bawl at Rome; Revolt and set up Popery at Home'.

In the context of increasing fear from the Church of England and Royalist interests that the days of 1641 had come again, Charles was given full support to execute all the Exclusionists implicated in the plot he could lay his hands on. The remnants of the Whig leadership either went underground or fled to the Continent. By late 1683 there was a severe purge of Whig and dissenting interests in the localities: as Charles II commented, 'for his part he would put down popery, but he would also have all the laws put into execution and none of the Dissenters spared.' The Exclusion crisis was dominated by anxieties about the relationship between 'popery and arbitrary power'. Sir Henry Capel put the thoughts of most Whigs succinctly: 'lay popery flat and there's an end of arbitrary government and power, it is a mere chimera or notion with out popery.' Opposition to the rule of James, and ultimately Charles, was shaped by the fear of popery derived from the cultural memory of the Gunpowder Plot. The fear of 'popery', then, was primarily a political problem.

It is remarkable that James II ascended the throne in 1685 with only the mildest of political turbulence – the 'Protestant' duke of Monmouth (a bastard son of Charles II) attempted unsuccessful military resistance in the West Country. Bloody Judge Jefferies dispatched the rebels with brutal punishment – the pickled quarters of the rebellious were sent to all parts of the kingdom as a warning of the consequences of sedition. Despite this secure succession, James II, in the view of the Protestant elites, reverted to 'popish' type, bringing tyranny and Catholic emancipation together in his pursuit of toleration. James took advantage of his legitimate regal prerogative and the supposed loyalty of the Anglican establishment to promote an extensive measure of liberty of conscience – for radical Protestants as well as Catholics. In this sincere act of tolerance the Protestant mainstream detected a plot – in fact, they saw evidence of the enduring nightmare of popery restored. Such power did the fear of popery wield in the Protestant mind that it was impossible to imagine liberty for Catholic worship without conjuring up images of conspiracy and persecution.

The Glorious Revolution of 1688–9 established the constitutional principle that political liberty could only be built upon the foundations of Protestant institutions in Church and state. The fact that the providential wind had protected the

The Papists Po

1588.

DEO Trin-VniBritanniæ bis ultori, In M
Proditionis Nefa
To God, In Memory of His double Deliverance fr
Dem Drey-Einigen Gott zu ehren; zur ewig
wirtlichen Span-ischen Armado, und der verstu

Difflo:
I blow and
Ick blaes en
ich blase und

Diffipo.
scatter
verstroy
zerstreue

Silury Campe

In perpetu

Ventorum
Ludibrium

In foream quan foderi
In die grub so sie g
werden fallen dise

Straverat innumeris. &c.

OCTOGESIMUS OCTAVUS, mirabilis Annus
Clade Papistarum, faustus vbique pijs.

Im Acht und Achtzigsten Jahr;
Alm Engelland erlöst war;

Perditione prius
Perditâ pe

Der rächterr
Luch und Plü

reason
lassis Invincibilis subversæ, submersæ;
æ dilectæ.
Navie, and yͤ unmatcheable Powder=Treason
einer Zwÿffachen errettung von der Gnüber=
Verrähtzerÿ

VIDEO RIDEO

Isee and smile; Ich sie en lach; Ich sehe vnd Lache

Jamiam

Opus tenebrarum.
A Deed of Darknesse.
Ein werk der finsternüs.

Novemb:

Quantillum absuit
Hoenae. How neare!
Ach wie nache!

Fauc.

Wir waren schon verloren gscheht
Doch hat es Gottes zug entdeckt

Invented by Samuell Ward preacher of
Ipswich.
Now repeated by a Transmariner. A° 1689.

ione, petebant;   Fausta et festa dies, Ev: Aurea QVINTA NOVEMBRIS
rodita proditio.   Anglis sulphureum prodidit illa nefas

ist,   Von Pulver=feür=vnd schweffel regen
Böllen=list.   Hat Gott errett' vns durch sein segen

Dutch fleet and brought William of Orange to Torbay on 5 November reinforced the belief that the watchful divine eye was protecting the nation from the Roman Antichrist. The spectre of French-sponsored military invasion in the interests of the deposed Stuart monarchy meant that the fear of popery remained a powerful political instrument for mobilizing national identity throughout the eighteenth century. The constitutional settlement of the Bill of Rights (1689) is drenched in anti-Catholic language. Reinforced in the Act of Succession of 1701, the point is that the constitutional framework of 'modern' Britain was shaped by fear of popery. Even the monarchy was subject to confessional limitations: it is still the case today that no prospective successor can either profess the Catholic faith or marry a Roman Catholic. Equality of opportunity, regardless of religious confession, does not, then, apply to the modern monarchy.

It was only a few years ago (1998) that an editorial in the *Catholic Herald* called for the end to Bonfire Night as an 'Incendiary remnant of a more volatile and believing age'. As the editorial insisted, 'The recent *auto da fé* in Lewes, in which "the Pope" was burnt in effigy, offended many Catholics and brought back talk of the "bad old days" before Catholic Emancipation.' As the paper went on, Bonfire Night was an offensive act: 'would loyal Anglicans wish to see Catholics burn the Archbishop of Canterbury in effigy . . . or, far worse, would they wish to see an effigy of the Queen, as Supreme Governor of the Church of England, burst into flames?' The editorial insisted that the persistence of the event was a constant reminder of the Protestant foundations of British culture, but that it also gave succour to paramilitary elements within radical Protestant traditions in Northern Ireland. Predictably, this plea for abandoning the tradition was rejected by radical Protestant communities. Catholic demands for curbing the burning of effigies of the Pope were reviled as an ignorant and typical distortion of the historical facts. History showed how – according to the Protestant view – Roman Catholics had consistently fomented military conspiracies against Protestant liberties – thus to some today, British history is a pageant of the success of the Crown and the People in escaping the tyrannies of the Papacy. Bonfire Night celebrations are, in this view, a necessary part of the public commemoration of the successful foiling of one such attack – the Gunpowder Plot – which aimed 'to change, alter and subvert the Religion here established . . . to ruinate the state of the Commonwealth and to bring in strangers to invade it'. It seems that, unfortunately, the fierce confessional passions of the seventeenth century are still with us.

CHAPTER FIVE

Bonfire Night in Lewes

MIKE JAY

On any other day but 5 November, Lewes is a sedate, historic and exquisitely pretty market town in a broad valley among the chalk downs of East Sussex, a few miles inland from Brighton. Yet on Bonfire Night – or 'the Fifth', as it is universally known in these parts – it becomes the scene of a dark carnival of fire and noise on a scale unmatched anywhere else in Britain, on any night of the year. Of the small handful of English towns and villages, mostly spread across the southern counties, that still celebrate the Fifth in the traditional manner, Lewes has long been the largest, the proudest and the wildest. A century ago it was already widely recognized as 'the strong citadel of Bonfiredom', where 'the celebration of the Fifth acts like a fever' and 'confusion reigns supreme in the old streets'. But the origins of the Fifth in Lewes, and the reasons for the full-throated and bloody-minded persistence of its celebrants, must be sought earlier still, in the extraordinary scenes of the years around 1850 that gave birth to the ritual so jealously preserved and spectacularly commemorated today.

The first intimations of the drama begin at dusk, as the cold of the early winter night descends. Visible between the shoppers in hats and coats hurrying up and down the steep inclines of the High Street are apparitions who seem to have slipped discreetly across the borders from another world. Whispering children in elfin cloaks and hoods dash in and out of each other's front doors; a stray cavalier in sumptuous ruffs and red satin pauses for a cigarette in a side street. A mustachioed soldier in pith-helmet and gold braid loiters, nipping at his hip flask; small groups of young men in blackface and hooped guernsey jumpers stealthily pull trolleys piled high with mysterious mounds, wrapped in tarpaulins and leaking petrol. Behind the scenes, the town is being mobilized on a scale rarely seen in peacetime, for an operation that will transform it from sleepy market town to temporary war zone. Paradoxically, it is precisely because Lewes remains a sleepy market town that its riotous bonfire tradition has survived.

It is not a single large-scale operation that is being mounted at this point, but half a dozen competing ones. Each district of Lewes and many of its outlying villages have their own bonfire society; each is massing in one or another corner of town, donning disguises and forming ranks for their grand procession, on which flaming torches, dazzling flares, marching bands and an aural assault of squibs, bangers and firecrackers will accompany them through the streets of their section of town. Let us follow the banners of the Cliffe Bonfire Society, whose domain is the quarter of town below the old bridge, backed up against the chalk cliffs that shear the valley from the high downs above and give the district its name. The Cliffe is the largest of the bonfire societies, the most breathtaking in artistry, and one of two that can trace their origins back to the years in the mid-nineteenth century when today's bonfire rite was first constituted. For more than 150 years, broken only by the odd typhus epidemic and two world wars, its procession and subsequent firework display have maintained and embellished a tapestry of rituals in which both the history and the myths of bonfire are ever more tightly woven.

Long before the Cliffe are visible through the crowds that pack the High Street, the fire from their torches ripples the night

air, smearing the outlines of the neat brickwork and half-timbers of the old town and illuminating the embroidered banner that hangs high across the narrow span, defiantly proclaiming 'No Popery' in squat red letters flanked by the society's skull-and-crossbones insignia. A distant cacophony resolves itself into the sound of bagpipes and marching bands peppered with an approaching firestorm of bangs, flashes and Chinese firecrackers reverberating off the shopfronts. The crowds part before the advancing wall of heat, light and noise, and the vanguard of the procession materializes through the smoke: massed ranks of full-bearded Vikings in tunics of furs and animal skins, faces hidden behind horned helmets of beaten copper glinting in the firelight, carrying petrol-soaked crosses ten feet tall on thick wooden poles, their fur-booted feet plodding determinedly under the weight. When their crosses are torched at the climax of the procession, the knowledge that the Vikings are a relatively recent addition to the scene – only introduced in the 1950s – does little to dispel the sense of a pagan rite dignified by antiquity, a blazing rebuttal to the death of the year in cold and darkness.

Behind the Vikings, the procession streams out of sight, a succession of torch-bearing battalions whose range spans continents and centuries in a bewildering and exotic masque. Victorian regimental uniforms of red and gold, tartan, bearskin- and pith-helmets, are interspersed with Royalists in wigs and brocade, sombre privates from the Great War and darkly elegant military dandies in skull-and-crossbones battledress. Giant Remembrance wreaths roll through, followed by bluestocking suffragettes whose banners proclaim 'Votes for Women', followed in turn by cardinals in tall mitres and blood-red cassocks. Weaving between each of these are the hundreds of Bonfire Boys and Girls, whose mufti of soot-streaked faces, black and white hooped guernseys, white trousers, red sashes and bandannas forms the backdrop to the tableau, and whose origins are inseparable from those of bonfire itself. The Bonfire Boys are both orderlies and mischief-makers, jaunting along beside the revenants of the past, swigging from kegs of scrumpy, nonchalantly distributing deafening squibs among the crowd, gathering up the flaming detritus of discarded torches and tossing them into the 'tar barrels' lugged by their fellows, oil drums cut in half and mounted on wheels that trundle and clank over the cobbles, constantly exploding with bangers that rattle shop windows and send chimneys of sparks high into the air.

The cavalcade's musical accompaniment matches its sights, a flux of precision and chaos. Several full marching bands are interspersed through the procession: jaunty ragtime brass, a bagpipe ensemble, military oompah, Boy Scout orchestras stumbling over burned-out debris as they read from the sheet music mounted in front of their noses, concentrating grimly on keeping in step and time. Tradition is seasoned with innovation: over recent years a drum troupe of PVC-wrapped goth fetishists and dreadlocked urban shamans have coalesced to fire-juggle and pound out their fierce tribal beats. But ever constant are the bangs and explosions over which all the music struggles to make itself heard, and which forces both participants and observers over a decibel threshold where loud detonations no longer startle, and where the relentless noise eventually produces a strange enervation, both thrilling and curiously calm.

For those watching this display it is immediately clear that, most unusually for such a sumptuous and spectacular event, the intention is not to please the spectators. The Fifth is for the bonfire societies themselves. Visitors are at best tolerated: those who find a Bonfire Boy engaging them in friendly conversation should check the pavement by their feet, where the odds are that a surreptitiously dropped squib is about to explode. Public explanations of the event tend to be perfunctory – officially, it's simply a commemoration of Guy Fawkes Night like any other across Britain – yet the procession teems with slogans and banners that proclaim other messages entirely, or develop the meaning of bonfire in unexpected ways. To the outsider, these can appear alarming: the profusion of anti-papist imagery raises the spectre of sectarian hatred, while the Cliffe's belligerent and skull-studded motto, 'Death or Glory', gives little reassurance against the possibility of violence and anarchy. Both sectarian prejudice and violent anarchy are indeed firmly rooted in the traditions of the Fifth; while both have become to some extent symbolic, the right to parade such incendiary symbols remains at the core of the modern celebration.

But there is more being remembered here than the Gunpowder Plot. A finely embroidered banner of William of Orange's landing in 1688 reminds us that the Fifth is also the anniversary of a tyrant deposed and liberty restored, and more recent commemorations such as female suffrage align this liberty with the twentieth century's progressive causes. Another solemn banner suggests, by contrast, a sectarian history even older and more bitter than Guy Fawkes: the commemoration of the Lewes Martyrs, seventeen local Protestant citizens burnt at the stake in the High Street under Queen Mary in 1557. 'Enemies of Bonfire' are paraded in effigy: local councillors who have attempted to curtail the celebrations, pigs' heads in riot helmets representing the previous year's heavy-handed policing, Home Secretaries who have attempted to make political capital out of deploring Bonfire Night. Slogans, banners and causes traverse the modern political spectrum from left to right and back again, while plainly uniting the procession that marches beneath them. There are contradictions here, but there is also a history within which they are all assimilated, and which offers the Fifth its continued *raison d'être*. As one of the most prominent banners announces

to a torch-lit and shell-shocked town, 'We Burn To Remember'.

The processions follow their designated routes from their home corners of the town through its centre, snaking past one another in cacophonic chaos, bands struggling to keep time as they weave through each other's ranks. The Vikings of the Cliffe cross paths with the Zulu vanguard of the Borough Bonfire Society, whose origins date back to the Boer War and whose feathered headdresses tower almost as high as the Vikings' crosses. All the processions intersect at the Lewes Martyrs' Memorial on the High Street, where Remembrance wreaths mark the focus for a mass conflagration of bangers, livid pink emergency flares and hand-held 'illuminations' of Catherine wheels. But this is not the end of the ceremonies, only the end of their beginning. Now the processions peel apart and head for their own turf, the fire fields on the edges of town where each will mount a firework display to outdo the others.

The Cliffe field was until recently a free-for-all, thousands of visitors packed tight in dark, muddy and drunken chaos, but after one too many knife incidents and rocket injuries it is once more strictly controlled: a semi-private celebration for the participants themselves. A bonfire the size of a house is set alight, the beacon towards which the Cliffe process through the darkness, now trailing behind them the giant effigies stuffed with explosives whose detonation will frame the display: a huge Guy Fawkes, an equally towering Pope and, dwarfing both and teetering on its flatbed truck, a topical centrepiece to stand as the emblem of the year. These are exquisitely sculptured tableaux, scabrously witty and casually obscene, in a line of descent from today's *Spitting Image* puppets to the James Gillray lampoons of their heyday. Some years' effigies are local in their targets, some international; they frequently combine twin themes to brilliant effect. Recent Fifths have seen President Clinton dressed as a Stars and Stripes superhero, 'Captain

Viagra', clutching a pendulous phallic missile decorated with the motto 'In Gob We Thrust' – and, in a nod to Gillray's famous image of Pitt and Napoleon, a demented President Bush gorging on a pie in the shape of the globe.

The sensibility is sharply defined but, once again, hard to contain within a modern political frame. Traditionally right-wing issues such as Brussels and farming, for example, have made regular recent appearances – EU Commissioners spattered in slurry, their arms embedded in cows' sphincters, and in 1992 a memorably quixotic John Major mounted on a dinosaur (from that summer's hit film *Jurassic Park*) and tilting feebly at the European flag. Yet in 2000, the year of foot-and-mouth disease, the target was Labour's pusillanimous failure to repeal Section 28, represented by a stern Gordon Brown spanking a stockinged and suspendered Peter Mandelson over his knee. The motto beneath this tableau, 'Don't It Make Your Brown Eye Blue', was typical in its insouciance, provocatively politically incorrect, but in the service of a defining politically correct cause. If there is any unifying theme in the centrepieces, and indeed in the event as a whole, it is the ridicule of authority, which knows no political favourites. It is a theme that the Cliffe cheerfully turn against themselves: their own officials, often the drunkest members of the crew, proudly sport pompous uniforms decorated with slogans like 'Chief Official Wanker'.

The sculptures are designed in tight secrecy by a fireworks committee, and the climax of the procession is the first sight that the Cliffe themselves have had of them. As they are led to their site of execution, and the procession breaks rank to become spectators, attention turns to a scaffolded gantry that stands ten feet high in the foreground of the display. When all preparations are complete, this is mounted by a robed figure bearing crook and mitre, 'The Archbishop of the Cliffe', and two accompanying 'bishops' in clerical dress, their protective welding-visors both indicating and inviting the ritual to come. Opening an ecclesiastical tome, the 'Archbishop' attempts to read a Latin Mass to the crowd over a deafening chorus of boos and chants of 'Burn the Pope!'; bangers and squibs rain onto the gantry from all sides, until the bishops become the eye of a storm of flashes, bangs and smoke. Through his ordeal by fire, clutching at his mitre, smoke billowing up through the cassocks of his fellow bishops, the 'Archbishop' proceeds through a litany – full of topical wit, though inaudible beyond the front row – of charges against Guy Fawkes, the Pope and the Enemies of Bonfire, interrupted by the rhetorical call of 'What shall we do with him?' and the ever more emphatic audience response of 'Burn him!'

When the hoarse spectators have reached fever pitch and the bishops can endure the assault no longer, the sermon is concluded and the display begins. Guy Fawkes, then the Pope, and finally the effigy of the year, become the centrepieces for a pyrotechnic performance of savage intensity. The scale, of course, is spectacular, but there is a brutality of intent that sets it apart from the usual grand public display. There are the conventional high, blossoming starshells trailing gold and silver showers, but they are framed by deafening bangs that shudder the ground for minutes on end and fusillades of retina-scorching magnesium flares that seem to rip the sky apart; each display is terminated with extreme prejudice as the centrepiece is detonated, ripped grotesquely limb from limb, its carcass left burning in tatters. It is a display that elicits not the typical response of oohs and aahs; this is rather the full-throated roar of satisfaction vented, a mob burning their enemies on a cold winter night. These days there is irony, to be sure, and a ribald hilarity that must have been present from the beginning; but beating beneath them still is the pulse that characterized the origins of bonfire. As a newspaper report observed more than

150 years ago, 'there is a strong dash of earnestness in the fun inseparable from this demonstration.'

It seems unlikely that celebrations of the Fifth in Lewes date back in any recognizable form to the Lewes Martyrs, or even to the Gunpowder Plot. Throughout the seventeenth and early eighteenth centuries the events of Bonfire Night are scantily recorded; across England generally the official civic observance became dutiful rather than enthusiastic, a courtly and parliamentary event rather than a popular one. It endured as a public holiday that united the Church, for which it affirmed the establishment against the Catholic threat, and the state, for which it commemorated the Whig triumph of 1688 in securing constitutional liberties. It was only in the second half of the eighteenth century, after the Jacobite Rebellion of 1745, that it began to chime with a new public mood that recognized the anniversary of the Gunpowder Plot as a time-honoured rallying point for a new sectarian venom against the assault on 'English liberties'. In the growing towns and cities it became a night where young men, particularly artisans and labourers, could let off steam – and bangers, crackers and squibs – under a patriotic banner, often with the implicit or explicit support of an anti-Catholic gentry.

Such was the case in Lewes, where by the late eighteenth century there were warning signs of Bonfire Night's potential to get seriously out of hand. In 1785 what the *Hampshire Chronicle* described as 'the greatest riot perhaps ever known at Lewes' began when a bonfire was assembled at School Hill in the centre of town, a large crowd of young men stoking it until it reached a ferocity that terrified the local residents. They complained to the magistrate, who read the Riot Act to the crowd and attempted to lead an effort to pull the fire apart; the crowd resisted, scuffles broke out, and the magistrate was knocked down and rolled into the river, accompanied by the 'firing of rockets, squibs, grenades etc.' The disorder persisted until midnight, by which time enough officers and Justices of the Peace had been assembled to disperse the rioters. Arresting them, though, was harder: in a pattern that would repeat itself for decades, many of them broke away and melted into the night, while others fought off the authorities to free their comrades before they could be secured and locked up.

This kind of disorder became widespread across England in the early nineteenth century, as Bonfire Night became one of ever fewer opportunities for the burgeoning 'lower orders' to vent wider social frustrations. The conscription and food riots of the Napoleonic Wars had produced new anxieties among the propertied classes about public order, and led to new emergency powers to maintain it; at the same time, the disenfranchised majority had become increasingly politicized by radicals like Tom Paine (who worked in Lewes as an excise officer in the 1770s, and is now the town's favourite son). As the gentry and leading citizens withdrew their support from the festivities, shadowy and anonymous 'bonfire gangs' came to fill the vacuum, collecting subscriptions, coordinating crowds and building bonfires and effigies. Particularly across southern England, the Fifth took on the character of a night of misrule, where masks were worn, dissent vocally expressed, authority figures parodied and their houses targeted with bonfires, tar barrels and rockets.

While such dissent plainly had a political dimension, it was an awkward fit with the nineteenth century's emerging political structures. By the 1820s, grass-roots campaigns for political reform – the union movement and, after the 1832 Reform Act, the Chartists – were determinedly shunning civil disobedience in favour of lobbying and peaceful demonstration: rioting, for them, was an unwelcome hangover from the mob violence of the eighteenth century, easily dealt with by the authorities and politically counter-productive. The causes of bonfire, in this context, were unsophisticated, amounting to little more than a right to make mischief: as one newspaper dismissed them, 'the lower classes absurdly consider the suppression [of bonfire] as an infringement on their rights as Englishmen.' Bonfire put down its deepest roots in rural market towns, typically in the southern counties, where industrialization, urbanization and working-class politics were at their weakest.

Nor was the energy of the popular demonstrations easily harnessed by either of the political parties. Their anti-Catholicism and patriotic commitment to Church and king were in the Tory spirit, but their unpredictable violence made them dangerous bedfellows for local grandees, and attempts to co-opt them for overtly political purposes could backfire in ridicule or worse. They also, on occasion, adopted unambiguously Whig causes: in 1831, after the Reform Act had been rebuffed at the first attempt by the House of Lords, the bishops who had voted it down became the year's most popular bonfire effigies. To the chagrin of politicians, what had become the most popular festival of the year in a huge swathe of England's heartland, from the Home Counties as far west as Devon, had turned politics itself into one of its most succulent targets.

In Lewes, the riotous celebrations were by now becoming more ritualized, and taking place on a disturbingly large scale. The shadowy coordinators, their identities frequently concealed with masks and blacked-up faces, were first dubbed 'Bonfire Boys' in 1827; in 1832, for the first time, blazing tar barrels were rolled through the streets and set in motion down School Hill, trailing incendiary debris behind them. When police attempted to seize the barrels, the Bonfire Boys turned the chase into a new sport and, in 1834, took to piling the barrels into a huge bonfire outside County Hall. The same year, in nearby

Brighton, when the High Constable attempted to suppress the revelry a stone-throwing mob smashed the windows of the hotel where he was staying.

In Lewes, as elsewhere, the Fifth was exposing and exacerbating an ugly rift that was developing in the town between the emerging middle class – propertied, often Liberal in politics, nonconformist in faith and puritan in inclination – and the agricultural and labouring poor, in their view asserting their traditional rights, covertly supported by the longer-established Tory and Anglican gentry. The struggle for control of the town on the Fifth became ever more hotly debated through the 1840s, and the celebrations ever more daring and dangerous. The flashpoint came in 1846, when 'disguised persons in several parties and accompanied by a large mob' opened the evening in now-traditional style by dragging tar barrels through the town to a large conflagration outside County Hall, after which they turned their attention to the house of the local magistrate, Mr Blackman. When Blackman emerged from his house and attempted to arrest one of the ringleaders, 'he received a blow over the eye from one of the bludgeons which was on the instant raised, and he was felled to the ground', and 'carried into the house in a state of insensibility'. The Bonfire Boys allegedly had no idea whether he was alive or dead, and little interest: the bonfires, squibs, rowdy singing and drinking carried on unabated for several hours more.

This incident was a trigger for the anti-bonfire party to mount what they saw as a long-overdue campaign to curtail the excesses of the Fifth in Lewes. A pamphlet entitled *Observations on the Doings in Lewes of the 5th November 1846*, signed anonymously by 'An Old Inhabitant', fired the first shot in a campaign that would build through 1847 to enlist the editorial support of the *Sussex Advertiser* and mount a petition to the Magistrates' Bench. 'Old Inhabitant' argued that the 'disgusting parade of disguises, bludgeon and riot' should now be consigned to the past. He could not imagine a more 'disgusting sight' than 'a large body of human beings in a state of savage excitement, slaves to the worst feelings and impulses of which their nature is susceptible', taking over the town with impunity in disguises that recalled 'the poison-cup and the stiletto of the Italian bravo'. In his view, the authorities had no choice but to 'adopt such decisive measures' as would thwart any 'unseemly proceedings' in the future. By September 1847 his sentiments had been echoed in a petition of thirty-two 'leading inhabitants', warning the local magistrates that 'we have great reason to apprehend that such riotous and tumultuous proceedings will be attempted upon the Fifth of November now next ensuing.'

The debate had bubbled all year, with local newspapers dividing along recognizable party lines: the Liberal *Sussex Advertiser* calling for the festivities to be suppressed, the Tory *Sussex Agricultural Express* deploring the excesses, blaming the volume of alcohol consumed and proposing a compromise: that the celebrations be moved perhaps to a less contentious site outside the town. From the Bonfire Boys themselves there had been silence, but few doubted that a show of strength was afoot, and they were to be proved right. At the stroke of midnight on 4 November, the rumbling of tar barrels was heard and a crowd of Bonfire Boys began their procession down the High Street, 'preceded by a man armed with a pick axe and disguised by a mask, and followed by about eighty others armed with bats and bludgeons, shouting and making an awful uproar'.

As ever, the local forces of law and order were outnumbered and outgunned. A handful of constables held a chain across the street; several Bonfire Boys fell over it, eight were arrested and the remainder scattered into the darkness. But the petitions to the magistrates had not been in vain: by noon of 5 November, eighty police had arrived on the train from London, and by dusk they had mounted a cordon in front of County Hall, where the crowd gathered for a stand-off. For a while they 'amused themselves with using insulting expressions towards the police and special constables, an occasional rocket being exploded in the thickest part of the crowd', but by eight o'clock 'a disposition was manifested by the crowd to go to greater lengths.' The Brighton mail coach arrived and attempted to make its way past the crowd, but a stray squib caused the horse to bolt. It ran into a shop front, to cheers from the crowd and another volley of squibs, and the magistrate and local landowner Lord Chichester hurriedly ascended the steps of County Hall and read the Riot Act. The police charged the crowd and, although several constables were seriously hurt in the mêlée, the crowd was eventually dispersed.

The London police were dispatched back to the capital the next morning; but although the Fifth was finished, the Bonfire Boys were not. That night, and every night for the rest of November, more than a hundred of them descended on the town to rampage. The streets blazed with tar barrels, the air cracked with fireworks, and those who had mobilized the campaign against bonfire were singled out mercilessly. The offices of the *Sussex Advertiser* were subjected to nightly assaults, 'which appear to have been expressly selected', as the editor grimly noted, 'with a view to retaliation for the remarks we have felt it our duty to make'. By the end of November the magistrates were forced once more to swear in special constables, draft in more police reserves and dragoon the town back to order. Once again, the Bonfire Boys proved slippery, their ringleaders impossible for magistrates to identify. Only four arrests were made, and the suspects were all eventually discharged, their defence solicitor arguing that the disturbances had been 'not what is ordinarily termed a riot, but . . . the keeping up of an old custom and might be regarded more as a frolic'.

The year 1847 had ended in a conspicuous triumph for the forces of bonfire, and one that would endure. Being drafted to keep law and order on the Fifth was no one's favourite detail: special constables were regularly fined for deserting their posts or refusing to serve in the first place. Furthermore, attempting to suppress the celebrations invited random and anonymous acts of retaliation: as the *Advertiser* observed, 'let any individual only be suspected by the mob as unfavourable to them, and forthwith he is a marked man – if he venture among them he is personally ill-used or insulted, or his house beset with tar barrels down to the front of it and burnt.' It seemed that the compromise mooted by bonfire's moderate supporters was the best solution, and in 1848 the crowd was led away from the High Street to the outlying Wallands Park estate, where they roared, sang, drank and exploded squibs and rockets to their hearts' content. The problem, it seemed, was solved, and the exercise was repeated the following year without incident.

In 1850, however, the story took the decisive twist that would produce the ritual of the Fifth as it is constituted today. Following the Catholic emancipation of 1829, the Pope had that year restored the hierarchy of Roman bishops in England, headed by a new archbishop of Westminster. This move was characterized in Anglican heartlands as 'the Papal Aggression', and the response to it was voluble, persistent and extraordinarily bitter. 'Protestant England', declared the *Sussex Agricultural Express*, 'is fairly aroused . . . we look with shame at the depth of degradation to which half-a-century of concessions to Rome has led us.' The prospect of the nation being 'parcelled out into Romanist dioceses' mobilized anti-papist sentiment to a degree that had not been seen for a century, and established a climate where the traditional affirmations of Bonfire Night were no longer too extreme but too mild. 'If all that we are doing', the *Express* concluded, 'is the burning of an effigy, or the shouts of a mob, Rome will regard it as no more than the flash of last year's rockets . . . this monstrous project must be defeated.'

All across southern England, the Fifth was celebrated in 1850 with unprecedented intensity, encompassing towns where bonfire had previously been restrained or entirely absent. In Farnham, for example, it was recorded that 'our usually quiet town was yesterday the scene of a most determined and universal, though pacific, "No Popery" demonstration.' In Brighton, there was a huge turnout, but the 'evening passed off better than usual'; the consensus was that attempts at suppression had made the disorder worse, and most concluded that 'forbearance on the part of the authorities is the better policy.' In Lewes, the Bonfire Boys seized their moment and returned to the town centre with a vengeance. The streets resounded with the blasts of the fat home-made squibs known as 'Lewes rousers', and for the first time the tar-barrel procession was set ablaze at midnight at the spot where the Lewes Martyrs had been burned at the stake by Marian papists. The current alarm was compounded with ancient history, and the celebration was taken to imply a permanent permission to return to 'old customs', an assertion of traditional liberties now regarded as dating back three centuries.

The following year, it was as if it had never been otherwise. 'The streets of Lewes', recorded the *Express*, 'presented the usual aspect: squibs and crackers were fired in all directions.' The Bonfire Boys roamed freely, and their 'blackened faces and ingenious disguises appeared to afford the highest amusement to the inhabitants'. For the first time, a separate celebration was noted on the far side of the river, where 'at Cliffe Corner a capital effigy of the Pope was consumed on a grand bonfire.' In the centre of the town proper, a theatrical flourish was added to the bonfire ritual: 'a figure dressed as a Romish priest', which was hailed with loud cheers by the assembled crowd as 'the Cardinal', accompanied by another figure in ecclesiastical drag acclaimed as 'the Pope', were strung up over the bonfire in front of the White Hart Inn and 'pelted mercilessly by squibs of all sorts and sizes, which came thicker and faster' from a crowd chanting the verses of 'Remember, remember the Fifth of November' or, as the *Express* drolly put it, 'loudly avowing their ignorance of any pretext for forgetting the existence of Gunpowder Treason'. Although the Pope-burning was an innovation, a topical response to the issue of the day, even on its debut it seemed deeply rooted in tradition, and it would rapidly become hard to believe that it had not always been an integral element of the night.

Many more elements of today's ritual were woven into the celebrations in the next two years. On the Fifth of 1852 'the town was speedily alive with squibs, crackers, rockets etc.', and at ten o'clock 'the great event of the night took place – the procession of the Pope and Cardinal Wiseman [the archbishop of Westminster] to their appointed doom.' This time they were accompanied by the first local Enemy of Bonfire: the editor of the *Sussex Advertiser*, whose name was Bacon, noted that 'an ingenious representation of the editor of this journal in the shape of a pig' was also consigned to the flames. Once more, at Cliffe Corner, 'a capital Pope was brought to the stake.' But at the time that these traditions were forming, they were still viewed as responses to a current emergency.

We have no doubt [observed the *Express*] that, by a conciliatory course, the time may come when the magic words 'Remember, Remember, the Fifth of November/Gunpowder Treason and Plot' may lose their spell, and the celebration may die out. But whilst Protestants are still languishing in Tuscan dungeons for reading the Bible to their maid-servants, surely the time has not yet come for abandoning one iota of our hostility to Rome.

What was not yet foreseen was that the truculent insistence on the right to bonfire itself would prove to be a far more enduring force than the immediate crisis that had restored it.

The following year more flourishes were added; the description of the 1853 celebrations, and even the panorama of them painted by Thomas Henwood, could almost stand for the event today. The threat of suppression seemed permanently on hold, and the Bonfire Boys were in full regalia, 'worn rather to give effect to the scene than a disguise'. The Enemy of Bonfire was for the first time an international one: with the Crimean War looming, the centrepiece proclaimed 'Down with the Czar', 'preceded by a large Russian bear, modelled with a degree of artistic skill' that made observers almost 'indignant at its transfer to the flames'. With the 'cheers, Rule Britannias, and the Guy Fawkes ditty, the banging of squibs, the sounds of the band, all mixed together, and forming an inextricable confusion of sound', the Pope, himself 'a finished work of pyrotechnical art', detonated at the climax of the ceremony. Across the river, the display mounted by the Cliffe was 'certainly equal, if not superior, to that exhibited in the town . . . amongst the banners figured the famous inscription, "No Popery" '. For the first time on record, too, the Cliffe had drawn a crowd of spectators 'from Brighton, and other places in the neighbourhood, who appeared to enjoy the event amazingly'.

This was the year from which the earliest bonfire societies – the Cliffe, and the Lewes town society now known as the Borough – officially date their formation. After 1853 their organizing committees, it seemed, no longer needed to hide in the shadows. Yet the bonfire wars were far from over, and within twenty years Lewes and a tight network of smaller bonfire societies in the surrounding Kent and Sussex borders, would be virtually the only ones left standing across southern England. The tendencies that had attempted to end the celebrations in Lewes in the 1840s were on the march across the nation: rural towns everywhere were becoming larger, better policed, falling more firmly under the control of a middle class for whom protection of property and security of public space were prevailing and increasingly dominant values. Bonfire riots spelled the end of the ceremonies across the Home Counties from Essex to Surrey. Guildford, for example, had long rivalled Lewes in the scale of its celebrations, but failed to maintain them against the new civic backlash. In 1863 the bonfire crowd's frustration burst its banks, and they set on a local magistrate's residence with hammers and axes, demolishing windows, doors and the entire front of his house; but this type of disorder was now more easily dealt with, and by 1870 'scarcely a squib' was in evidence across the town.

There is no single or definitive answer as to why Lewes in particular stood firm against the tides of history. Part of it must be that, unlike towns such as Guildford that expanded in size and industry, Lewes remained a relatively small market centre, with much of the local population growth gravitating to nearby Brighton and Horsham. But a major factor seems to have been the local bonfire party's highly effective mix of intransigence and strategic compromise. On the one hand was the opposition's fear of reprisal from an event they had failed to suppress in the past, and to which the events of 1850 had given a greater public legitimacy; on the other were negotiated settlements between the civic authorities and the newly visible bonfire societies, who offered concessions such as planned procession routes and designated bonfire spots that contained the free-floating disorder.

This spirit of compromise may have built on a particular local tradition of negotiation that had been glimpsed previously in the agrarian 'Captain Swing' riots of 1830 that swept from Kent across the south coast to Sussex, then up through the Home Counties to Huntingdonshire and beyond. The Swing riots were brutally suppressed – nineteen public executions, and more than 500 collaborators transported to Tasmania – but in Lewes, despite a large constituency of labourers 'very active in promoting discontent and tumult', they were resolved peacefully in a mass public meeting: the largest local landowner, Lord Gage, met with a deputation of tenant farmers on Ringmer Green, and agreed to their demands to reduce rents so that they could pay higher wages to their labourers. The rioters of Lewes had abundantly demonstrated their ability to play hard cop, but they had experience of playing soft cop too.

By the late nineteenth century, once the Fifth in Lewes had weathered the anti-bonfire storm, it was increasingly hailed as a cherished institution and a quirky display of civic pride. Although it maintained its trademark denunciations of popery, the new causes it adopted were in tune with the prevailing imperialist mood, celebrating Britain's colonial adventures in India, Egypt, Afghanistan and South Africa and pillorying Liberal leaders for their opposition to them. In 1875 the *Daily Telegraph* reported with admiration on the 'people wonderfully dressed' beneath 'the great No Popery banner, attended by the Society's brass band', and the climax where once 'the bishops had read a mock service and delivered up a fiery exhortation, the three gigantic effigies were brought up, amid howls and execrations.' Tussles over the legitimacy and ownership of bonfire continued – Temperance activists campaigned against it, Orange lodges attempted unsuccessfully to appropriate it – but by the early twentieth century it was widely felt that the celebration 'was shorn of all real religious significance long ago . . . it is a survival and a revival of those old-time demonstrations against Romanism, which were the excuse for a licence for men to lose their reason for a few short hours in the year.'

This opinion was offered by the journalist Arthur Beckett, whose fond pursuit of the 'old-time flavour' of the Sussex Downs generated pieces for the *Spectator*, the *Idler* and the *Field* that were published in book form in 1909 as a series of 'impressions and reminiscences' of the area. Beckett's reportage of the Fifth in Edwardian times combines benign nostalgia with a sharp sense of the continuing dangers of the event. 'The hooligan element is in strong force,' he warned; 'it is better to carry a stout stick than to go unprotected.' He further recommended that 'it is well to wear old clothes and to cover the eyes with wire goggles against stray sparks . . . it is a wonder no-one is crushed to death, as the object of the Lewes Bonfire Boys is to spread confusion, and confusion reigns supreme in the old streets of Lewes for some eight or ten hours.' Nevertheless, 'to the man unacquainted with Lewes, the spectacle of a sleepy town run mad on one evening of the year is a matter for marvel.'

The fireworks are over, and visitors are being crammed like sardines onto the special late trains back to Brighton and London; but the final, most private and most potent act of Lewes's ritual is still to come. Back in the centre of town, ankle-deep in firecracker debris drifting like autumn leaves, the bonfire societies are regrouping, bangers and crow-scarers once more rallying their straggling marches back to their respective strongholds. Here, torches are piled on the sites of the original nineteenth-century bonfire spots, forming burning mounds around which the Bonfire Boys reassemble and the bands reform. At Cliffe Corner, Vikings mingle with cavaliers and bishops, hip flasks and scrumpy kegs are drained and impromptu tea-stands steam the greasy night air. The Cliffe sort themselves into the best approximation of the early evening's procession they can muster, and the company sets off for a last march around the town, bangers emptied from pockets into tar barrels and rubbish bins, explosion after explosion setting off shop fire alarms in their wake as, drunk on fire and noise, they claim the streets once more in celebration of their traditional rights.

In every corner of town, the same acts are being performed: figures in cloaks and masks scurrying or staggering through side streets to bonfires where their societies are congregating. The brave, the drunk and the foolhardy leap over the fires to the cheers of their comrades, usually avoiding anything worse than minor burns, though serious accidents at this point are not unknown. Each year at Lewes brings its crop of battle-scars – rocket-burns, eye injuries, hair set alight by falling firework debris – yet, perhaps remarkably, there has been no direct fatality of the Fifth since 1909. There is much experience and fire-sense behind the apparent recklessness, and everyone knows the emergency drill if you fall into the flames: hold your breath and roll out.

Up and down the bombed-out streets, muttered chants, rousing choruses and barrages of firecrackers echo through palls of smoke. At Cliffe Corner, watched by crushes of revellers hanging from the open windows of the flats above, hundreds jostle around the bonfire for the concluding Bonfire Prayers. The moment is jealously guarded and, when necessary, fiercely defended. In the early 1990s Vikings often tangled with officious riot police; around the same time, the insensitivity of a magic-mushroom- and alcohol-addled traveller contingent led to several ill-tempered stand-offs and eruptions of violence. The Cliffe have shared the rest of the night with the police and the crowds, but its final moments are theirs alone. 'Please to remember the Fifth of November' starts up, everyone from

children in pageboy ruffs to old-timers in tattered military braid
barking their way through verses long forgotten elsewhere:

> Burn him in a tub of tar
> Burn him like a blazing star
> Burn his body from his head
> Then we'll say old Pope is dead
> Hip-hip hurrah!

The brass band segues into 'Rule Britannia', 'God Save the
Queen', 'Land of Hope and Glory' and 'Auld Lang Syne'; a
hand-held setpiece is sparked up, spelling out 'Good Old Cliffe'
in fizzing Catherine wheels; Bonfire Boys and Girls pair up
and sidle away; the final bangers and crackers are dumped on
the fire in a shower of sparks, and the Cliffe's ceremonial fire
engine, a quaintly restored Victorian gurney, pumps an ironic,
token splash of water onto the flames. The Fifth is over for
another year; the preparations for the next will start almost
immediately. The work of bonfire is never done, and the struggle to maintain it against rising tides of regulation, policing and
local complaints demands constant vigilance. But it is a struggle
to which the bonfire party of Lewes has been committed for
generations, and one which has in its time subsumed many
other struggles and causes. The language of Gunpowder
Treason may have been written over repeatedly, but it has not
been obscured; rather, it has become a palimpsest in which the
history of Lewes is etched in ever finer detail.

CHAPTER SIX

Making Fireworks

BRENDA BUCHANAN

'when all the fire is lit and the guns go off, and the rockets, fire tubes, squibs, and balls go hither and thither nothing can be seen but smoke and fire, and verily it seems then to be the fire imagined in hell'

Vannoccio Biringuccio, *Pirotechnia* (1540)

Bonfire Night owes its special place in English life and history to the events of four hundred years ago when king and Parliament came close to being destroyed in a massive explosion of gunpowder. But the celebration of that deliverance has shifted over the years from a focus on the perpetrators of the plot, echoed in the name 'Guy Fawkes Night', to the observance of a more general festival in the cycle of the year, coming between Harvest Festival and Christmas and referred to uncontroversially as 'Bonfire Night'. This secularization of the Fifth of November not only allows it to be celebrated without any religious bigotry, it also enables it to be placed firmly in the context of the historically long-standing and geographically widespread celebrations involving bonfires, coloured smoke, sparkles and bangs. These extravaganzas preceded the mid-ninth century AD discovery of gunpowder in China, but then absorbed that new and powerful feature into the range of celebrations. At times such as the New Year, for example, the Chinese would welcome the occasion by throwing bamboo on a fire. When heated, the air within the bamboo exploded with a loud crack – giving rise to the name *pao chang* or 'firecracker'. But when gunpowder was discovered and became available, it was packed into the bamboo tube and *yen huo*, a 'firework', was created. Thrown on the bonfire as tradition dictated, the explosion would be even more exciting. As fireworks developed, even the Chinese court was not immune to the panic they might cause. At an indoor display in 1264 the empress-mother was sufficiently frightened by an 'earth rat', *ti lao shu*, a tube of bamboo filled with gunpowder that rushed around on the ground, that she stood up, 'gathered her skirts about her', and ordered the festivities to stop.

Seen in this historical context, as in its later manifestations, gunpowder is ethically neutral. It may seem fitting that the saving of the establishment from the murderous intentions of the gunpowder-plotters should be celebrated by gunpowder-fireworks, but against the unholy trinity of 'Gunpowder Treason and Plot' of the old rhyme must be set the progressive trio of 'Gunpowder, Compass and Printing Press', long held to be significant forces for good in the world. In an argument that remains familiar, gunpowder owed its place in this pantheon to its perceived contribution to peace, for it was thought to be so devastatingly and destructively powerful that it would end wars – no sane person would do battle. Sadly, it was clear by the early seventeenth century that this was not the case, but the neutrality of gunpowder if not its place among the virtues was preserved, for despite its use by man as a tool of aggrandizement and oppression, it came to be valued for its role in the development of mining, trade and settlement, and in national and private festivities.

Gunpowder-making is more of a technology than a science. It is concerned with the mixing together in varying proportions of three basic ingredients: saltpetre, sulphur and charcoal. Of

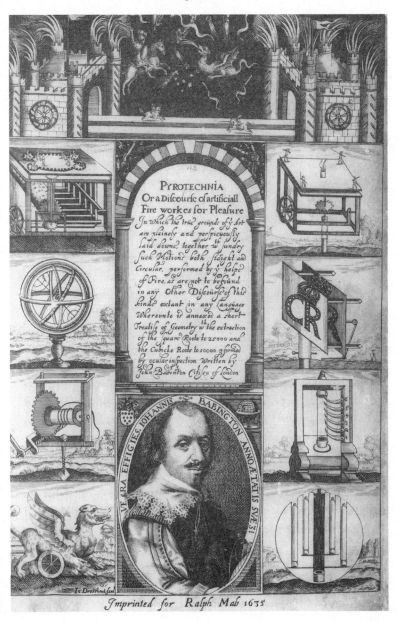

PYROTECHNIA
Or a Discourse of artificiall
Fire workes for Pleasure
In which the true grounds of y^e Art
are plainely and perspicuously
laid downe, together wth sundry
such Motions both straight and
Circular, performed by ye helpe
of Fire, as are not to be found
in any Other Discourse of this
kinde extant in any Language
Wherevnto is annexed a short
Treatise of Geometry wth the extraction
of the Square Roote to 25000 and
the Cubicke Roote to 10000 performed
by ocular inspection Written by
Iohn Babinton Gunn^er of London

VERA EFFIGIES IOHANNIS BABINGTON ANNO ÆTATIS SVÆ 31

Io. Droeshout. sculp.

Imprinted for Ralph Mab 1635

147

these, saltpetre (potassium nitrate) is the most important in terms of proportion and significance, for it provides the oxygen necessary for the flame to take hold when the mixture is fired; sulphur's contribution is to permit combustion at a lower temperature than would otherwise be the case; and charcoal, with the sulphur, provides the essential fuel.

Gunpowder was becoming known in Europe from the mid-thirteenth century, but its manufacture was little understood. The English writer John Bate described it in poetic words in 1634: 'The Saltpeter is the Soule, the Sulphur the Life, and the Coales the Body of it . . .' More prosaically, the fundamentals of the subject were summed up in the opening lines of a paper presented to the Royal Society of London by Thomas Henshaw in 1662 and published in 1667. Here, the essence of the process is shown to be the incorporation of the three ingredients with such thoroughness that a grain of gunpowder would then contain each in its correct proportion. This degree of incorporation would not be achieved by a casual stirring – it required a firm mixing under pressure. This was first done manually with a pestle and mortar, but from at least the sixteenth century this tiring process of limited scale was mechanized by the harnessing of animal- and water-power. The contents of rows of mortars were pounded by banks of stamps descending rhythmically, but the very vigour of this operation carried the danger of over-heating and explosion, and so in 1772 stamps were outlawed in Britain except in the special circumstance of the production of very fine powder. They were replaced by heavyweight vertical edge runners, at first of stone and then of iron, that trundled over a curbed bed, grinding, mixing and compressing the ingredients – on the principle of the rolling pin rather than the pestle. Neither method involved a chemical transformation, and so in the early days the lightly 'mealed' or 'serpentine' powder would over time and during transit separate out again into its original ingredients. From the fifteenth century this disadvantage was overcome by 'corning', a practice by which the dampened incorporated powder was pressed through a sieve. The consolidated grains, resembling grains of corn, were then dried and proved – by simple processes that grew more sophisticated over time. There were to be further refinements and improvements, especially as with a growing expertise it became possible to regulate the force of the powder by varying the proportions used in the recipe and the size of the grains produced. But although the basic stages of gunpowder-making remained the same for war and peace, the military advances were not necessarily adopted for all festive fireworks. For example, corned powder could burn too rapidly for display purposes, and so a fine mealed powder remained in use for some of these occasions; and charcoal could be less finely powdered to produce a good display of sparks as a rocket rose in the sky.

A persistent problem over the years was that of storing gunpowder. The system in Britain, by which the Board of Ordnance relied (until the second half of the eighteenth century) on powder purchased from private manufacturers, provided some opportunity for regulating supplies. Nevertheless, there were always considerable stores held in and around London: at the Tower from the earliest gunpowder times, at Greenwich from the late seventeenth century; and at Purfleet from the 1760s, together with unknown quantities in the hands of private manufacturers and merchants. The danger of an explosion was ever-present. In 1584, for example, the Privy Council ordered that forty lasts of powder (each of twenty-four barrels or 2,400 lbs), stored in a house on Tower Hill, should be moved because here 'rogues and vagabonds oftentimes lodge in the night and burn straw to warm themselves.' But as well as the visible danger of sparks and fire, there was also the more insidious one of damp and decay, by which gunpowder could be just as effectively disabled. The high proportion of potassium nitrate in gunpowder makes it very hygroscopic or moisture-absorbent. The enemy is not floodwater, though that may have played a part in the decay of gunpowder in the holds of ships at sea, but atmospheric damp, present in many storage places, especially cellars. Oak barrels, each holding a 'short' hundredweight (one hundred pounds), or less commonly a proportion of that, offered some protection, and their ease of handling meant that they could be turned over regularly to prevent the formation of damp clots of powder; but the problem of deterioration remained a challenge. In this respect, corned powder was an improvement upon mealed or serpentine, but it still permitted the spread of moisture, a deficiency that was not addressed until the introduction of hand-operated screw presses, probably in the early eighteenth century. The more dense structure that resulted gave some, though still inadequate, protection against damp.

This problem has a particular relevance to the story of the Gunpowder Plot, for, as shown by the records of the Board of Ordnance, the powder that was recovered from the cellars of Parliament was 'decayed'. The Debenture Book (WO 49) reads:

From the Parliament Howse Septimo die Novembris 1605 anno Regni Regis Jacobi tertio Receaved into his Majesty's Store within The office of The ordenaunce from out of the vault undernethe the Parliament howse Corne powder xviii hundred weight decaied which was there laide and placed for the blowinge up of the said howse and destruction of the kings Majestie, the nobilitie, and Commonaltie there assembled. Receaved as aforesaid Corne powder decaied: xviii hundred weight.

This account shows that the powder had been corned, and so it is unlikely that the grains would have separated out into the three ingredients, the fate of the earlier, serpentine powder. But it would have remained susceptible to damp, and it was

probably this factor which led to its decay, rendering it un-
usable. Blowing up king and Parliament with damp, clotted
gunpowder, even eighteen hundredweight of it, would have
been a difficult proposition.

As already mentioned, gunpowder was in all probability first
discovered in the mid-ninth century in China. It is likely this
came about in the course of the search by Taoist alchemists for
the tantalizing but unattainable elixir of life. Materials would be
collected, refined and experimented on in simple laboratories,
and it was only a matter of time before the three ingredients of
gunpowder were mixed together and inflamed, with exciting
results. It hardly needs saying that combustible materials were
long known to be capable of *burning*, the distilled petroleum
or naphtha of Greek Fire being especially feared in sea battles
from the seventh century AD, but the early gunpowders, even
those with a low saltpetre content, had the added power of
deflagration, that is, of a sparkling combustion and a 'whoosh'
like a rocket. As the saltpetre content was increased, the
mixtures developed propellant qualities, capable of projecting
rockets and incendiary smoke balls. With a yet higher proportion of saltpetre, an *explosion* could be achieved in an
enclosed container, capable of bursting its walls and sending the
contents flying.

By the mid-eleventh century we have the first written
formulae for gunpowder in a Chinese treatise, the typical proportions (saltpetre 50.5% : sulphur 26.5% : charcoal 23.0%)
suggesting the manufacture of a weak explosive. Over the years
the saltpetre proportion was increased in both the civilian and
military fields, but with different aims. The visiting Jesuit priest
Pierre d'Incarville, for example, writing on Chinese fireworks
in 1763, noted in his account of 'Chinese Fire' that a saltpetre
proportion of 86.6 per cent was used for the finest floral effects,

and 60.6 per cent for the coarsest. But the military was not about creating wonderful effects – the aim was in general that of producing a strong and destructive powder. For this purpose in Britain, a standard ratio (saltpetre 75% : sulphur 10% : charcoal 15%) was established from the 1780s, which upon firing would produce a 'brisant' or violent explosive power. A lower rate of saltpetre, in the low 60s per cent, was used in mining for blasting purposes, so that the rocks might be shaken but not shattered. Grain size was also significant: it must be matched to purpose as gunners and miners had to learn, and used to produce different effects in firework displays as d'Incarville observed.

The debt owed to China covers not only the recipes for gunpowder, but also the inventive proliferation of many sorts of festive fireworks. Instructions written towards the end of the sixteenth century, for example, in Shen Pang's *Yuan Shu Tsa Chi* (1593), refer to 'resounding bombs', 'ascending fires', 'breaking waves' (which gave several explosions in mid-air) and the 'earth rats' already described. There are variations in packing – loose or tight; in the release of sparks – many or few; and in the wrapping or enclosure used – layers of paper to form tubes, or baskets and bowls. Chinese manuals also contained advice on the different colours which may be given to smoke and flame by the addition of natural and chemical substances – for example, in the fourteenth century indigo for blue-green, cinnabar for purple, and lignite and soap-beans for black. To achieve the greatest effect, many of these varieties of fireworks were gathered onto a single wooden framework, a temporary structure that was later to reach its greatest extravagance in Europe, where it was known as a 'machine' – something made to support a grand display.

Fireworks changed little over the years, and many of the differences of construction, content and effect have been simple

figure 12

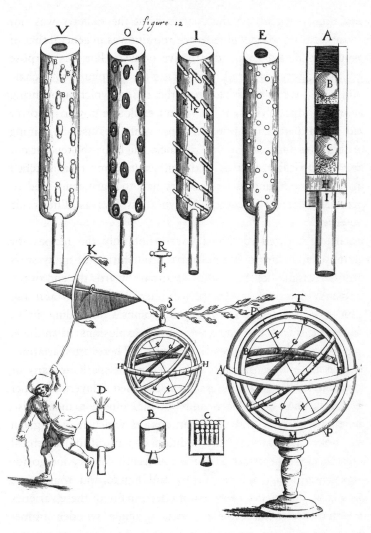

variations on earlier practice. Most were composed of a case capable of closure, a firework mixture, and a method of ignition. The exception was the 'sparkler', beloved by children of a less safety-conscious age because this was the firework that could be held in the hand. It was made of a piece of wire six to nine inches long, coated with a pyrotechnic mixture that produced a shower of sparks when ignited. Whirled at arm's length it produced a pretty and innocent effect. But in general there were cases, usually made of paper, cut to the required dimension and then 'sized' with starch or flour paste. While still pliable the sheet was wrapped several times around a 'former' or 'rowler' to produce a tube of the required dimensions that hardened as it dried. The use of an appropriate paper for a particular design was important: that for rockets, and for Roman candles packed with alternating layers of gunpowder and high-rising stars, must be strong enough to withstand high pressures and temperatures; that for the whirring pin or Catherine wheel must have a good wet strength so that the tube packed with powder could be dampened again to wind round the centre of the firework; that for lances with their white or coloured fire must be capable of withstanding the rough handling that was to become an inevitable part of their use in creating portraits and messages. In addition, the paper tube must be capable of burning at the same rate as the mixture it contained or the effect would be spoilt. For displays requiring rapid ignition a 'quick match' was used – a regular fuse encased in a tube designed to keep up the temperature so that a near-simultaneous ignition of many fireworks could be achieved.

The need for a rocket to achieve 'lift-off' made this firework a special challenge: gunpowder was pressed into a tube and a long conical central hole was drilled into the mixture, which was retained in position by a clay plug or 'choke'. When the rocket was ready for firing, steadied by a stick in an upright position in a container, the fuse was lit and the gunpowder in the tube burned rapidly outwards from the surface of the conical cavity. The internal pressure exerted force towards the upper end of the rocket, as the gaseous products of combustion escaped through a hole in the choke at its base. The rocket, guided by its stick, was propelled upward with its familiar 'whoosh'. The tube was usually designed with a cap or head, separated from the main body and containing a further 'bursting' charge of powder. When fired by a time fuse at the apogee of the rocket's climb, this released pellets of pyrotechnical material in the sky. At a firework display this may be called poetically a 'garniture of stars'; in early battles in China, and with lime mixed with explosive, it may be called a 'lime-fog', blinding men and horses.

There has been a remarkable consistency in the ingredients of the propellant charge since at least the accounts by English writers John Babington and John Bate in the early seventeenth century, with a preference for mealed rather than corned powder, and the addition of extra charcoal to the basic recipe to slow down the rate of burning, provide more fuel and add the drama of sparks to the rising rocket. The power needed to get the rocket aloft limited the amount of pyrotechnical material available for release. To remedy this deficiency, large numbers of rockets were employed at a time, with several thousand fired in quick order at great displays in the past, to create the spectacle of a 'bouquet of rockets'. In pursuit of a more effective individual firework there were experiments in England from at least the 1630s, with 'balloons' or 'bombs', later known as 'shells', fired from mortars. These were made of canvas of eight or nine thicknesses, and contained a slow-burning composition and a garniture of materials for a shower of stars. The mortars were not necessarily the military type, but might be 'pasteboard guns' strapped upright to a plank of wood. The shell was placed in the mortar with the fuse pointing down into a lifting charge

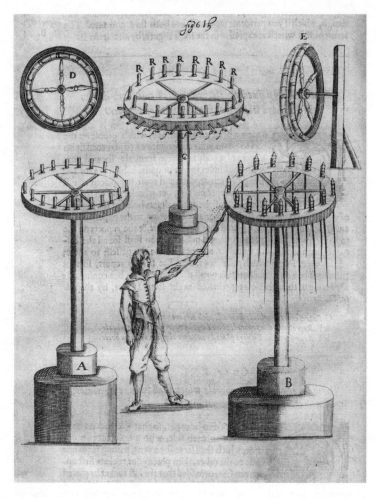

of loose gunpowder that was fired through the touch-hole of the mortar. At the experimental stage the advice of John Bate, 'And while that burneth, retreat out of harm's way', would have been sensible, but by the end of the seventeenth century shells were coming into common use in displays as they were able to carry a more effective 'payload' of pyrotechnic material than the rockets.

It is appropriate to mention here the only comprehensive treatise on civilian pyrotechnics in Chinese literature, the *Huo Hsi Lüeh (Treatise on Fireworks)* by Chao Hsüeh-Min. This mid-eighteenth-century work was not printed until 1833, but it was known and appreciated by Chinese scholars, and by Westerners who learnt many of its secrets through Pierre d'Incarville's paper of 1763. Chinese skills in colouring flame and smoke were noted earlier, but these now also included arsenical sulphides for yellow, cotton fibres for violet, verdigris and indigo for green, lead carbonate for lilac-white and pine soot and pitch for black smoke. But there were by then comparable developments in Europe: the French chemist Jean Appier had suggested the use of verdigris for a green coloration in the 1630s, and by the mid-eighteenth century powdered zinc was being used to produce a greenish-blue. An account written in 1845 by Claude-Fortuné Ruggieri, of the great family of Italian pyrotechnicians, then working in France, described many chemicals that have continued in use: barium for green, calcium for orange, copper for blue, sodium for yellow and salts of strontium for red. Until the middle of the nineteenth century Chinese fireworks continued to be regarded by many as the best in the world. However, a coming shift in the rankings was suggested by the fact that 'Chinese Fire', in which flame and smoke were illuminated by numerous silver sparkles derived from ground cast-iron (a triumph unknown in the West before d'Incarville's mid-eighteenth-century account), would be

transformed in brilliancy after 1860 by the European addition of magnesium and aluminium.

A knowledge of gunpowder-making was carried to the West as part of the diffusion of Chinese learning in the twelfth–thirteenth centuries, but a focus on the path to Europe places us in danger of overlooking China's nearer neighbour, India. There have been claims as to the primacy of India in the making of gunpowder but, unlike China, India's largely oral traditions were set within a mythical period of time and are therefore difficult to substantiate. But there are written accounts of firework displays in the fifteenth century, and lists of the materials used to produce special effects. A poem of 1570 refers to rockets and other fireworks producing garlands of flowers, sprays of fiery sparks, the effect of moonlight, and hissing noises. Of greatest significance, however, is the fact that after its 'launch' in China it was in India rather than Europe that the rocket came to prominence, despite its abortive use as a weapon in the naval battle between Venice and its rival Genoa at Chioggia in 1380. In China, the rocket was an aerial adaptation in the later twelfth century of the 'earth rat'. When a carton of gunpowder was attached to an upright bamboo cane, or the cane itself filled with gunpowder, the lighting of the fuse transformed the ground-sizzling version, which had caused panic at court, into a 'meteoric ground rat', a rocket. These were used in festive ceremonies, where as well as leaving the ground they could also travel along wires to light a glittering display of fireworks; but by the mid-fourteenth century a more serious military purpose was also being served, in campaigns to protect boundaries and control inland rebels and coastal pirates.

Despite this, rockets achieved their greatest early prominence when they were adopted in India, being employed there in battle from the fifteenth century. As an eye-witness of the battle of

Samugarh of 1658 suggests, the damaging effect of this 'granado fastened to a stick, that may be cast very far through the cavalry, and which extremely terrifieth horse, and even hurts and kills' was great, but it was the later use of heavier rockets against British troops in Mysore at the end of the eighteenth century that led to their incorporation into Western warfare. They were described in 1790 by a Scotsman, Quintin Craufurd, as an eight-inch tube of iron, one and a half inches in diameter, closed at one end, and packed with powder in which a 'match' or fuse has been inserted. This cylinder was strapped to one end of a four-foot length of bamboo, pointed with iron. The effectiveness of this weapon depended not only on the speed with which it went off, but also on its own deficiencies, for 'By the irregularity of its motion, it is difficult to be avoided.' So impressed was Craufurd that he showed these rockets on the title page of his book on Hindu history and learning.

In Europe, the early and rapid development of the gun meant that the rocket, this lightweight, transportable weapon of war, was largely overlooked, although simple rockets were making their contribution to firework displays. The use of the rocket for both festive and military/scientific uses came together through the efforts of Benjamin Robins in London in 1749, at the celebration of the Peace of Aix-la-Chapelle. In the previous year Robins had received the Copley Medal of the Royal Society of London for his work in the new science of ballistics, and he now took the opportunity presented by the massed flights of several thousand rockets to try to measure the altitude reached by these great formations. A colleague was stationed on top of a house some 4,000 feet away, and together they were able to calculate that, as Robins reported to the Royal Society some weeks later, the crest of the arch formed by the rockets was over 600 yards (1,800 feet) in altitude. Robins went to India in 1750 as the engineer general of the British East India Company, but died of a fever a year later. His scientific research was cut short, but one of his colleagues at the peace celebrations, the military engineer and army officer Thomas Desaguliers, appointed chief fire-master at the Royal Laboratory at Woolwich in 1748 and later its superintendent, undertook much valuable research there, including the earliest experiments with military rockets. However, he died in 1780, before the use of rockets in Mysore in the 1790s that so impressed the British soldiers.

The challenge of developing rockets for military use was shouldered by William Congreve the younger. He was to succeed to both a baronetcy and the post of Controller of the Royal Laboratory on his father's death in 1814, but in 1804, holding no official position yet having his father's support and royal approval, he began privately to experiment with rockets. These quickly went into production at Woolwich, where in 1806 the pasteboard tube of the firework was replaced by the iron casing or carcass observed in India. The rockets were initially put to use for ship-to-shore bombardment, perhaps most dramatically against Copenhagen in 1807 during the Napoleonic Wars, when the capital city of Denmark was greatly damaged by a flight of 25,000 rockets; and against Washington, DC, and Fort McHenry, Baltimore, during the Anglo-American War of 1812–15. Still a novelty, Congreve's impressive device gained the accolade of inclusion in the American national anthem with its reference to 'the rockets' red glare, the bomb bursting in air'. The difficulty of achieving accuracy by control-ling the trajectory of individual rockets, instead of impressing by mass-effect, meant that the military career of the Congreve rocket was chequered. Yet it remained in service until the 1860s, and proved a life-saver in many shipwreck dramas.

After this example of pyrotechnical diffusion via India, we turn to a second route by which the knowledge of gunpowder

and fireworks reached the Western world, through Arab inter-
mediaries. Here the great treatise on the subject is that by
Hasan al-Rammāh, written *c.* 1280 but drawing on the knowledge of earlier generations. It includes more than a hundred
recipes for gunpowder, suitable for military use and civilian
fireworks. The latter in particular show Chinese influence, with
references to 'wheels of China' and 'flowers of China', the inclusion of arsenic sulphide, lacquer and camphor in the mixtures,
and the use of expendable birds to carry incendiaries. From
the thirteenth century the knowledge and use of gunpowder
spread in the Mamluk kingdom (Syria and Egypt), along
North Africa, and across to the southern European borders of
the Mediterranean world, especially the Moorish kingdom
of Andalusia, and so into Christian Spain. Fireworks were a
familiar part of festivities in Arab cities, and it is even reported
in a treatise written in the second part of the thirteenth century
that at Hama in central Syria, Christians and Muslims together
celebrated the birth of Jesus with fireworks. These occasions
have remained a very vivid part of celebrations in rural Spain,
with fireworks made locally by craftsmen using ancient
techniques.

A third route of transmission concerns the traffic between
Europe and China, especially those travellers who returned with
treasures including information on the making of gunpowder
and perhaps specimens of the powder itself. They were not
many, but they are significant for the story of fireworks in
the West. They included military men, craftsmen such as gold-
smiths, merchants and churchmen – and it is likely that the friar
Roger Bacon of Oxford, the first person in Europe to write
about gunpowder, gained this information from a returning
cleric whom he met in mid-thirteenth-century Paris, then
the leading centre of culture and learning. His treatises, *Opus
Maius* (1267) and *Opus Tertium* (1268), reveal his practical

knowledge, and, although he refers disarmingly to children's toys, the fact that he writes of the violence of a combination of saltpetre, sulphur and willow charcoal shows his anticipation of trouble ahead. He notes that, placed in a parchment container no bigger than one's thumb, the roar as of strong thunder and the flash brighter than the most brilliant lightning would be very alarming. If the powder was placed in a larger container this noise and light would be difficult to withstand; and if a more solid receptacle was used the violence of the explosion would be even greater.

This was clearly written by someone who knew what he was talking about, which means that the interpretation of encoded information in his *Epistola de Secretis Operibus Artis et Naturae*, the *Letter on the Secret Workings of Art and Nature*, should have raised no problems. Instead, as well as questions of date and authenticity – certain passages may have been added later by a different hand – the proportions revealed when the code was cracked at the beginning of the twentieth century present another difficulty: saltpetre 41.2% : sulphur 29.4% : charcoal 29.4%. The low level of saltpetre may have made it difficult to achieve even a weak explosion, but this inadequacy can be turned to advantage as an argument in favour of authenticity, for some early recipes are known to have had a low nitrate content, later increased by practice and to suit different purposes. Was this information written in code to protect mankind from the perils of gunpowder, or was the need for secrecy a more personal matter? The latter was probably the case because Roger Bacon's interest in experimental science and technology led perhaps inevitably to brushes with papal authority, and the years before his death in about 1291 were spent under some kind of house arrest. Perhaps early gunpowder's association with alchemy and the references to its manufacture as the 'Black Art' did not soothe the worries of the papacy. The image of a powder-maker in the late-fifteenth-century Frankfurt *Rust und feuerwerck buych* (one of the many copies of the medieval German Firework Book), suggests that more than two hundred years later the alchemist still had the power to unsettle. The master is shown in a striped 'lab coat', surrounded by the apparatus of his craft and the signs of the seven metals. Although the text of the Firework Book is not mysterious, for it simply sets out clearly the system of question and answer by which the apprentice learned the craft of making and using gunpowder, the image is arcane, and it may have been the association with alchemy that led the Church to put an end to Roger Bacon's active interest in pyrotechnics. However, this third avenue by which the knowledge of gunpowder-making had been carried from China to the West, was by then becoming well established.

Until the middle of the nineteenth century no distinction was drawn in British administration between military fireworks to serve the national purpose on the battlefield, and festive fireworks for national celebrations – the Board of Ordnance was responsible for both, those 'for Real' and those 'for Triumph'. This was appropriate, because the grand public displays in honour of royal occasions and military victories marked dynastic and national success in a way that echoed, through the bangs and flashes of gunpowder, the same message of power as that conveyed by the gun on the battlefield. Not only were these public displays on an immense scale, so that great resources of technical expertise, artistry and design, finance and manpower, had to be brought to bear upon them, but they were also, unlike the pure spectacle of modern displays, designed to convey a message. Like theatrical productions they had a 'script', a story to tell.

One of the earliest of these great stage sets in Europe was

created in Stuttgart in 1609, in celebration of a dynastic coup: the marriage of the duke of Württemburg, a small duchy, part of the Holy Roman Empire, to the margravine of Brandenburg. A mock-fortress was placed on top of a small and specially constructed mound. Flames rose above it and fireworks filled the sky, but the sanctuary remained intact, protected by its position and by one figure from the rustic past, a 'wild man', and by two from the classical tradition, Mars and Venus, on lofty columns. The marriage would provide safety and security, the 'script' appeared to say. But as time went on the celebratory pieces lost their freshness and became so heavily allegorical that 'programme notes' were needed for their interpretation. By the time of the celebration in 1730 of the birth of the French dauphin a year earlier, the single mound had become two mountains, each eighty feet high, built in the space between the Pont Neuf and the Pont Royal in Paris. Given as a tribute by Philip V of Spain, these represented the Pyrenees: above them rose the sun, symbolic of the birth of the great grandson of the Sun King, and linking them was a rainbow on which sat the goddess Iris. This was a spectacle with action, for in the course of the display fireworks erupted around and between the mountains and sea monsters cavorted. If the omens of birth seemed obscure, no doubt all was made clear by the accompanying programme.

But the most skilled fire-workers over these years were Italian, and the most stylish firework displays were in the Italian cities, especially Rome. Vannoccio Biringuccio, quoted in the epigraph to this essay, was able to refer to the displays in Siena, his birthplace; Florence, where his shifting fortunes took him at one time; and Rome, where he was familiar with one of the city's great specialities, the 'girandole'. This was a spectacularly large wooden frame to which many rockets and other fireworks were attached, often so placed that they quickly lit each other in turn.

In Rome the opportunities for powerful displays were even greater than elsewhere, because the presence of the Holy See and the international network of diplomats, churchmen and scholars in attendance made this the greatest religious and secular city in Europe. The many celebrations included not only those of the Christian year, especially Easter, but also the annual display from Castel Sant'Angelo, which was so closely associated with stunning displays of rocketry that it became known itself as the 'Girandola'. The English painter Joseph Wright of Derby, famous for his depiction of light and luminosity, was drawn to paint this 'sublime' spectacle several times on his only visit to Italy in the mid-1770s, and his work shows smoke erupting as from a volcano, fireworks bursting and cannons firing. These displays were truly projections of great but graceful power.

England was not lacking in the opportunities for similar but smaller events, and after Queen Elizabeth showed her pleasure at the display commemorating her visit in 1572 to Warwick Castle, home of the Master General of the Ordnance, such occasions were repeated. This informal association between royal firework displays and the office of the Ordnance became well established, so it was appropriate that, after the disruption caused by the Civil War, the celebration of the coronation of Charles II in April 1661 should be designed by military engineers including Martin Beckman, a Swedish captain with Dutch forebears. Samuel Pepys noted that 'the City had a light like a glory round about it, with bonefyres' on the night of the coronation; he was sorry to miss the fireworks the next evening, but he was at home 'writing up three days' diary'. The coronation of James II in 1685 presented another major opportunity, and Beckman now mounted a water-borne display: there were barges on the Thames supporting mortars for firing 'balloons', musket barrels for firing 'stars', and 'triumph guns', as well as pyramids decked with fireworks; and there were 'water works' in the Thames, fireworks designed to impress by burning in the water. The occasion was a great success but it lacked the finesse and scale of the Continental displays, organized by men for whom pyrotechnics had become their sole profession. Beckman, on the other hand, as well as negotiating his way around the changing allegiances required by the return of the monarchy in 1660, the accession of James II in 1685 and of William and Mary in 1689, with all that this implied in dynastic and religious choices, was also much involved in making and using fireworks for war as well as for celebration. He served several times in Tangier, part of the dowry of Charles II's queen, and was closely involved in the establishment of this early British foothold outside Europe in the 1660s, as well as the destruction of its fortifications in the 1680s when the outpost could no longer be sustained. Appointed engineer to the Ordnance in 1670 (and living in the Tower of London from that time), Beckman became Chief Engineer in 1685 although he had fulfilled that role in all but name since 1677, touring the country and recommending and rebuilding its neglected defences. He was knighted for these services in 1686.

As another national crisis loomed through the efforts of James II to extend the Roman Catholic influence, a son and heir was born to the king in 1688, displacing his elder daughter, Mary, princess of Orange, and ending hopes of a peaceful Protestant succession. Beckman was called upon to produce a firework display to mark the birth of the baby who was never to become king, but would be known instead as the 'Old Pretender'. It took place in June, on the Thames, and the centrepiece was a statue of Cupid bearing aloft the three feathers of the prince of Wales. The landing of Mary's husband, William of Orange, in November, and departure of James and his family in December, threatened Beckman's position. But the Lutheran, having resisted the pressure to convert to Roman Catholicism, now felt it wise to ally himself to the Church of England. Perhaps his Dutch origins also helped, and he survived to present what must have been a hastily organized firework display on the Thames in November 1688, to welcome William, the new master. Contemporary prints suggest this was a splendid but orderly affair, in contrast to the more lavish display organized by the English merchants in Amsterdam, whose exuberance must have reflected their conviction that the Glorious Revolution was going to be good for them and for business.

Beckman's display may have been more tentative because he had much to lose. In addition to his role at the Board of Ordnance, he had also in August 1688 been made 'Comptroller of the Fireworks as well for war as for triumph and of all the fireworkers ... in the Laboratory' at Greenwich, an appointment which placed him in charge of the establishment where military and display fireworks were produced, and where he had already given long service as a firemaster since 1661. He retained both posts and received fresh warrants, proving his loyalty to the new regime by the active service he undertook, in Ireland in 1691 and in the bombardment of the French coast between 1692 and 1697.

As chief engineer, Beckman's prime task was to shore up the home defences, so his visit to Ireland was brief, but as Comptroller of the Laboratory he was to spend several years working on 'bomb vessels' sent to 'insult the coast of France'. He saw service at sea in 1692, and again in 1694 in an expedition to Brest, but his 'machines', fireships designed to explode near other vessels or harbour walls, were not a success. In 1695 he played his part in attacks on Dieppe, Le Havre and Calais, with bombs fired from ships at sea. Getting close enough inshore was difficult, but Beckman had an unorthodox success in 1696 when he hoisted French colours while manoeuvring ten 'bomb vessels' into position, to bombard Saint-Martin on the Île de Ré. The action lasted for two days and was followed by a further bombardment along the coast at Olonne. In all, '4,200 bombs and carcasses were thrown to good purpose.'

What were these 'fireworks'? Reference has already been made to 'bombs' fired in festive displays – hollow canvas shells filled with powder and a garniture of sparkling effects. In military service the bomb, also known later as a 'shell', was a hollow iron shot carrying a pyrotechnic composition, fired from a mortar. It had a fuse-hole about an inch in diameter, through which the powder was loaded and the fuse placed. The flash, as the mortar was fired and the shell expelled, carried to the fuse, igniting the powder in the shell and causing it to burst, as timed, against sea or shore defences. The 'carcass' was also a hollow iron shot, but oval in shape, and with up to five holes primed with powder and 'quick match'. Inside its ribs of iron it carried a highly explosive and incendiary mix including mealed powder, broken glass and such inflammable materials as pitch and turpentine. Discharged against a town, it created an intense fire, difficult to put out. Alongside this deadly work, Beckman served the king with a firework display to mark his safe return from the Continent in November 1695 after the capture of Namur, and rounded this off in 1697 with an extravaganza to celebrate the Peace of Ryswick and the successful conclusion of the Nine Years War.

The death of Sir Martin Beckman in June 1702 ushered in a quieter period of firework activity that lasted for more than forty years. There was no great public display at the coronation of Queen Anne in April 1702 – perhaps Beckman was already ailing at his home in the Tower. The ships at Spithead made a brave show at night, 'hanging out candles [in lanterns] as thick as possibly they could be hung and some firing several sky rockets', but as at the later coronations of George I in 1714 and

George II in 1727 there seems to have been no national focus, although there were reports in the *London Gazette* of 'bonfires, illuminations, ringing of bells and other demonstrations of a general satisfaction and joy'. On the Continent, royal events continued to be handsomely celebrated, but in Britain, during the generally peaceful years of Sir Robert Walpole's administration, the principle of 'Let sleeping dogs lie' ruled, and activity at the Laboratory in particular was greatly reduced. When national interests were felt to be threatened by Spain, leading to the conflict in 1739 which merged into the War of Austrian Succession (1740–48), steps were taken to remedy the Laboratory's 'defective state', although not until 1746 was it again placed under a 'Comptroller'.

Charles Frederick was the young man appointed, and he had yet to prove himself because unlike Beckman he had no successful military career to call upon as evidence of his abilities. Like Beckman, however, he was to hold positions for nearly forty years at both the Laboratory and the Board of Ordnance, where he was appointed Surveyor General. He was similarly to be associated with military success, for it was on his 'watch' that Britain emerged in the course of the Seven Years War (1756–63) onto the world stage as a naval, colonial and trading power. A Member of Parliament with influential friends, Frederick's personal advantages were a practical and well-organized mind and a willingness to learn about gunpowder-making. By Order in Council from the Court of St James, February 1746, he was appointed Comptroller of the Laboratory so that 'the Art of making Fireworks for real use as well as for Triumph may again be recovered.' His staff was to include a chief firemaster, firemaster's mate, clerk and workmen – especially the *matrosses*, who were to produce fireworks and cartridges and to charge bombs, carcasses and grenadoes at what, having moved downriver from Greenwich in 1696, was to become known as the Royal Laboratory at Woolwich.

Two years after Frederick became Comptroller the War of Austrian Succession was over, and, having been appointed to make fireworks for war rather than triumph, he was now required to change his priorities. It was decided to hold a firework display of previously unmatched splendour in London to celebrate the Peace of Aix-la-Chapelle, but just as the country had lagged behind its Continental neighbours in acquiring the skills of gunpowder-making, so also the staging of displays lacked the flair and intensity of meaning of those in mainland Europe. Italians were therefore invited to design the framework (Giovanni Niccolò Servandoni, architect and fireworks master) and the fireworks (Gaetano Ruggieri, forebear of the famous pyrotechnic firm), but the supply of gunpowder and the making of the fireworks was to be in the hands of Charles Frederick and the Royal Laboratory at Woolwich. He threw himself into the project with great vigour, working in an office set up for him at Green Park where the spectacle was to be held. He was described by gunpowder-makers who had dealings with him, as a man who had 'studied his Art [in this context, his technical skills] more than any Man in England, and made more Experiments'. Those who knew him socially marvelled at his intense commitment to the task: his sister-in-law reported that 'He is in the Green Park from 8 in the morning till 4 in the afternoon . . . The rest of the day he gives audiences and worries his spirits and his person till 'tis reduced to a shadow'; and a visitor to his office described him, alarmingly, as 'bronzed over with a patina of gunpowder'. While Frederick tackled the fireworks, ably assisted by Captain Thomas Desaguliers, the chief firemaster, the Italian pyrotechnicians worked on the setting, an edifice of wood and canvas, 410 feet long and 114 feet high, whitewashed and sized so that it looked like the finest stone. This was known as the Temple, or more technically the

'Machine'. The chosen site was close to St James's Palace, then the home of the Royal Family. Along Constitution Hill, the Royal Train of Artillery was to be drawn up to add the boom of cannons to the bangs of fireworks. As well as the myriads of ground-based fireworks, a great flight of over 10,500 rockets was to be deployed, serving, as already noted, a scientific as well as a festive purpose, for their trajectory over London was to be calculated.

The preparations begun in November 1748 culminated in the display on 27 April 1749. At seven o'clock in the evening the king led out the royal party, and, to a background of music played by George Frederick Handel and his orchestra (later to give his specially composed 'grand overture on warlike instruments', accompanied by a hundred brass cannon), he inspected the arrangements and distributed bags of gold in what were to prove premature rewards. At half past eight a signal rocket was fired, setting off a response from the guns in the enclosure, the cannons on the more distant hill, and then the fireworks themselves in great and rapid profusion. There were some mishaps, especially when one of the rockets struck a young woman spectator who had to be stripped to her 'stays and petticoat' so she should not be burned, and the thought that Charles Frederick may have 'over-egged the pudding' comes to mind as the problems of conflicting lines of command and methods of approach began to emerge. He was in overall charge, but the Italian experts were responsible for lighting the fireworks on the machine, and this they chose to do by laying a trail of corned gunpowder rather than the 'quick match' favoured by the home team as a safer and more rapid approach. Perhaps due to this confusion there was an explosion at the northern end of the machine, which burst into flames. Water engines were brought to the scene and the fire was eventually extinguished and the display resumed, but not before the

The GRAND WHIM

Being the Night View of the ROYAL FIREWORKS, as F
and the cutting away the two Middle Arch

OSTERITY to Laugh at:

the Green Park, St. *James's*, with the Right Wing on Fire,
nt the whole Fabrick from being Deftroy'd. 27ᵗʰ *April* 1749.

Cavaliere Servandoni, incensed at the spoiling of his machine, had drawn his sword and confronted Charles Frederick in anger. He was disarmed and dispatched to the Tower, to be released the following morning after apologizing to Frederick.

Firing was resumed after these incidents, but by midnight the crowd was drifting away and the celebrations came to an end with many fireworks left unused. These were employed a few weeks later in a second display at the Thames-side home of the duke of Richmond. There is a dramatic series of engravings of the calamity in Green Park, but the Richmond print has a special attraction for around the edges it shows and names the various fireworks used. They include a 'Fixed Sun', a 'Regulated Piece of 5 Munitions', a 'Buitoni', which looks like a bundle of fireworks on a stick, a 'Vertical Wheel', a 'Spiral with Horizontal Wheel', a 'Vertical Sun', a 'Battery of Maro[o]ns', 'Pots d'Aigretts with Fountains', 'Corded Mortars with Air Balloons', 'Do. With Saucissons', 'Flights of Sky Rocketts', 'Pots de Brin', 'Water Rocketts', 'Jatte d'eau', 'Water Balloons with 3 Stages of Lights' and 'Vertical Illuminations' – this last referring to four very substantial obelisks packed with fireworks.

As a spectacle the Green Park extravaganza was clearly flawed and there were few attempts to repeat a display on this scale, but it was a bravura performance that marked a revival in the fortunes of the Royal Laboratory at Woolwich and the Board of Ordnance. For more than half a century the emphasis would be on fireworks for real rather than triumph, as Britain began to assert its pre-eminence on the world scene, and supplies were pre-empted by the coming struggles for European, colonial, naval and trading power. There were celebrations to come, honouring for example, on the evening of 1 August 1814, not only the signing of the Treaty of Paris on 30 May that year (concluding, it was hoped, the struggle with Napoleon), but also the centenary of the House of Hanover on the British throne, and the sixteenth anniversary of the battle of the Nile; and Queen Victoria's many anniversaries were celebrated over the years following her coronation in 1838. But those of 1856 marking the end of the Crimean War were to be a 'last hurrah' for the military pyrotechnicians, who seem to have thrown everything they had into this final display. With four separate shows to accommodate the crowds, that at Green Park seems to have had a particularly spectacular conclusion, an eye-witness describing a complicated centrepiece which, 'amid all its fantastic blazing and revolving, exhibited the words "God Save the Queen" '. He continued,

Language fails to convey a vivid idea of the deafening, roaring, crashing and grand appearance of the termination, during which the proud fortifications of Sebastopol were supposed to succumb. Then rose up into the blackness . . . rapidly one after another, six flights of rockets, comprising altogether no less than ten thousand of these beautiful and brilliant instruments . . . It was such a spectacle as a man could not reasonably expect to witness more than once in his life.

This echo of Sir Charles Frederick's similar grand flights of rockets in Green Park a century earlier marks the successful conclusion of one hundred years of international rivalry. Indeed, as the remnants of the firework displays were returned to Woolwich by the waggon load, the Royal Laboratory found that it was being placed on a peacetime footing with the loss of 300 workers. Not only that, the long-standing link between the Ordnance Department and public fireworks was to be severed. It was perhaps in an act of neat but unsuspecting symbolism that much of the now redundant equipment, such as the special 'wire wound mortars', was to be sold to the fireworks firm of C. T. Brock & Co. The Victorian public was not to be deprived of its pyrotechnical joys.

*

A VIEW *of the* FIRE-WORKES *and* ILLVMINATIONS, *at his* GRAC[E]
Perform'd by the direction of Charles Frederi[ck]

Fix'd Sun.

Regulated Piece of 5 Mutations

Brulons.

Vertical Wheel.

Spiral with Horizontal Wheel.

Vertical Sun.

Battery of Marons.

Pots d'Aigrette with Fountains.

N°1. Pavilion beautifully illuminated.
2. The Duke of Richmond's House.
3. The Boats and Barges, for the
Aquatic Fire-workes.
8. His Majesties Barge.

Vûe des FEUX-d'ARTIFICE et des ILLVMINATIO[N]
sur la TAMISE et vis a vis de son

Conted Mortars with Fir Ballons
D° with Serpents

Flights of Sky Rockets

Pots de Brin

Water Rockets

Salte d'eau

Water with 3 Stages   Ballons of Lights

Vertical Illumination

1. Le Pavillon magnifiquement Illuminée
2. L'Hotel de Monsg.r Le Duc de Richmond
3. Les Bateaux employées aux Feu d'artifices Aquatique
4. Barque de sa Majesté

ar Monseigneur le Duc de RICHMOND de LENOX et d'AUBIGNY.
adi le 15.ième de Mai 1749. Sous la direction de Mons.r Frederick a Londre

The mid-nineteenth-century acquisition of first-rate fireworks equipment by the Brock family firm was particularly appropriate, as they had been associated with these celebratory materials from the early eighteenth century. Indeed, the death by fireworks of an ancestor, John Brock of Clerkenwell, in an explosion at his house on 5 November 1720, is particularly significant, for the date indicates both the long-standing family interest in this dangerous business, and the availability of gunpowder for private celebrations on Bonfire Night. This raises the question of the sale of powder for such purposes, and the legality of its non-military use.

The evidence is patchy, but it seems that from the sixteenth century there was a growing use of fireworks that were, in the words of the mayor of Bristol in 1574 when anticipating a visit by the queen, 'devised for plesure'. The date is of interest because this is only two years after the display at Warwick that had so pleased Elizabeth and which, through its association with the Ordnance, was interpreted earlier as setting a pattern for future state celebrations. But perhaps her enthusiasm also set the scene for civic displays such as that at Bristol, which lasted three days and involved artificial forts and mock battles, the purchase of corned and serpentine powder, and the casting of seven mortars of brass with the necessary pestles, presumably for the better incorporation of the ingredients of gunpowder. And it was not only the queen who enjoyed gunpowder displays on her tours of the kingdom; there is also evidence of the purchase of smaller quantities of gunpowder by colleges, guilds and borough councils for use in their various pageants and processions, such as that still associated with the Lord Mayor of London's Show.

The availability of gunpowder for these 'plesures' in the sixteenth century presents a problem, for this was a time when the government was still heavily dependent on northern Europe for supplies of gunpowder materials and expertise. There was such a lack of home competence in the production of saltpetre that a contract was entered into in 1561 to gain this knowledge from Gerard Honrick, a captain of 'Almayne'; and it was only from this time that the supply of gunpowder by contractors began to be organized. Even then, production was limited and largely confined to the London area, which suggests that the provincial guilds and boroughs may have bought supplies from illicit powder-makers, like those known to have operated in Bristol, or have 'acquired' them from royal castles in the country. With the sailing of the Spanish Armada in 1588 the shortages of supply became dangerously evident, and in January 1589 royal letters patent for gunpowder-making and saltpetre production were granted to a partnership led by the Evelyn family and held by renewal for almost fifty years. Given the Spanish challenge, it is no surprise to learn that in 1587–8 the merchants of the Mercers Guild in York had difficulty buying corned powder and match for their Midsummer Show. It is also no surprise that the goods were then purchased in Hamburg, and that this or another order was brought in on board the *Elizabetha* of Hull, for the wealthy merchants of the time were familiar with such overseas markets. The fact that similar displays were recorded at Bristol, Chester, Canterbury and Maidstone suggests that similar conditions existed there. Many of these pleasurable diversions were celebrations of English themes, often including St George and the Dragon, spitting fire from throat, nostrils and eyes, propelled by rockets and enlivened by an assortment of other fireworks. Nevertheless, this pyrotechnical freedom in the provinces sits oddly with the problems of supply in the metropolis and the perceived dangers to the state.

The middle decades of the seventeenth century were a difficult time for the pursuit of pyrotechnical pleasures, not through

gunpowder shortages but because of the condemnation of such frivolous activities by the new Puritan rulers. With the return of the monarchy in 1660 the theatres flourished once more, and the idea of 'Pleasure Gardens' began to take root, in London particularly. Here the shows were enlivened by fireworks, sometimes used cruelly – the 1710 programme at the aptly named Bear Garden in Clerkenwell, for example, refers to bull- and bear-baiting, and the dressing up of a dog with fireworks. The more 'select' establishments, such as the Mulberry Gardens, later the site of Buckingham Palace, and the Marylebone Gardens, would celebrate the king's birthday with firework displays. Cuper's Gardens south of the Thames also became a very fashionable resort where Handel's compositions were performed, and where in 1749 and 1750 a miniature version of the Green Park 'machine' for the peace celebrations was reproduced. Perhaps the most fashionable were the Ranelagh Gardens, which flourished from the 1740s until their closure in 1803, their grounds becoming part of the Chelsea Hospital; and the Vauxhall south of the river, probably the 'Foxhall Spring Gardens' known to Pepys. The Vauxhall closed in 1859, with the words 'Farewell for Ever' appearing in the final display in letters of fire. The opening of the Crystal Palace at Sydenham in 1854 had challenged the old London gardens and many could not survive the competition, especially when this was followed by the development from 1865 of purely pyrotechnic rather than scenic displays there. In the provinces there were a number of gardens famous for their firework displays, especially the Belle Vue Gardens in Manchester, the Spa in Scarborough and gardens such as the Sydney and Grosvenor in Bath, where a dreadful accident showed the price to be paid if things went wrong. Giovanni Invetto was a skilful and inventive pyrotechnician from Milan, but in 1789 a fireworks explosion at his lodgings in Bath caused the death of his wife and son.

Accidents highlighted the need for legislation and its enforcement. This was slow to come, but in the course of the eighteenth century regulations were introduced to govern the storage and carriage of powder and even the method of production when, as noted earlier, stamps used to pound the ingredients were outlawed in 1772. But it was not until 1875 that the control of explosives was placed on a proper footing, and even then the continuing exclusion of Crown property left workers at factories where military explosives were made, such as the Waltham Abbey Royal Gunpowder Mills, in a vulnerable position. Action was taken more quickly to control what might be regarded as the lesser hazard of letting off fireworks in public, perhaps because this could lead to disturbances that were difficult to control. At the end of the seventeenth century the sentiments were anti-popish, though these may equally have been expressed on Queen Elizabeth's Day, 17 November, the anniversary of her accession, rather than on Guy Fawkes Night, 5 November – which as a further complication was also sometimes celebrated as the day on which 'The Deliverer', the Protestant William of Orange, had landed in 1688. In 1685, troubles on 5 November were sufficient to cause the authorities to promulgate an Order in Council on the 6th, warning against bonfires and public fireworks on any festival or other day without permission. The troubles must have continued, because this Order was reinforced in 1697 by an Act of Parliament whose prohibitions included not only the firing and throwing of 'Squibbes, Rockets, Serpents or other Fire-works' in public streets, but also the making and selling of the same. The Act remained on the Statute Book until 1860, yet it was possible during that time for gentlemen of means to buy books of instruction such as that by Robert A. Howlett, entitled *The School of Recreation: or a Guide to the Most Ingenious Exercises* ... Published in 1696 and reprinted in 1710 and 1736, it

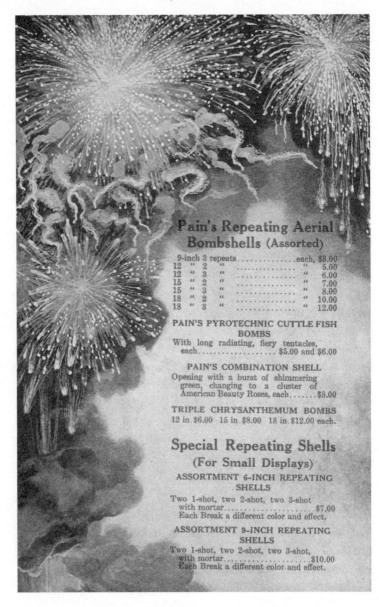

Pain's Repeating Aerial Bombshells (Assorted)

9-inch	3	repeats		each,		$8.00
12 "	2	"			"	5.00
12 "	3	"			"	6.00
15 "	2	"			"	7.00
15 "	3	"			"	8.00
18 "	2	"			"	10.00
18 "	3	"			"	12.00

PAIN'S PYROTECHNIC CUTTLE FISH BOMBS

With long radiating, fiery tentacles, each.................. $5.00 and $6.00

PAIN'S COMBINATION SHELL

Opening with a burst of shimmering green, changing to a cluster of American Beauty Roses, each....... $8.00

TRIPLE CHRYSANTHEMUM BOMBS

12 in. $6.00 15 in. $8.00 18 in. $12.00 each.

Special Repeating Shells
(For Small Displays)

ASSORTMENT 6-INCH REPEATING SHELLS

Two 1-shot, two 2-shot, two 3-shot with mortar...................... $7.00
Each Break a different color and effect.

ASSORTMENT 9-INCH REPEATING SHELLS

Two 1-shot, two 2-shot, two 3-shot, with mortar...................... $10.00
Each Break a different color and effect.

gave advice not only on such country pursuits as hunting and hawking, but also dealt in very great detail with the making of fireworks for pleasure.

Howlett's instructions for making fireworks such as 'Red fiery Stars', and 'Girondels or Fire-Wheels', would have required an investment in tools and materials. It was the simple and accessible squib that was the great leveller, and feared as such. In accounts of 'Tumultuous Disorders' on the streets, on Bonfire Night and other occasions, this was the firework that seems to have caused most trouble. In 1678, for example, there are references to 'the numerous platoons and volleys of squibs discharged'. The squib was simply composed of a small, strengthened paper tube, perhaps like Roger Bacon's child's toy, packed, though not too tightly, with gunpowder; and ignited by a fuse. It was troublesome to the authorities because it could be so easily made, perhaps with gunpowder taken home from an authorized factory or other place of legitimate use. Yorkshire miners, for example, made squibs for blasting by filling rolled paper tubes with powder, and these could then easily be used for domestic purposes such as cleaning chimneys, or on Bonfire Night. As a variation, a smaller, powder-filled and flattened case could be bent into a zigzag to make a 'Jumping Jack', known abroad as an 'English Cracker', perhaps because of its disorderly use in this country. When fired at one end and thrown to the ground there would be a small explosion at each bend of the tube, and the 'jack' would jump about alarmingly. The image of the unpredictable squib or jumping jack, fizzing, squirming and jumping along the ground with the crack of small explosions, takes us back to the beginning of the firework story, to the *ti lao shu*, the 'earth rat', which had so alarmed the Chinese empress-mother in the mid-thirteenth century.

*

Fireworks provide us with a very unlikely window on the world. Through this we can look back to ancient China, India, the Arab and the Western worlds, to see the close conjunction of alchemy, the experimental method and technological processes; we can be puzzled by a product that can be at once so destructive but also give so much delight; which can be used to celebrate public events by imparting a message of power, but is also capable of great spectacles 'devised for plesure'. There can be changes of scale as well as of function: the squibs in the streets, and the modest fireworks and bonfire in the back garden which delighted so many families in the twentieth century, before the present greater emphasis on safety obliged us to return to the public celebration of Bonfire Night. Above all, these fireworks for 'triumph' enable us to place in human perspective the dreadful power of the fireworks for 'real' – it was after all that later empress-mother, Victoria, whose portrait in lights at her Jubilee on a machine 200 feet long and 180 feet high, included fireworks which to the consternation of the pyrotechnicians refused to behave with propriety, so that her aerial image winked beguilingly at the crowd. But, spectacular as they are, such firework celebrations are of a transient nature, designed for a special occasion. Only Bonfire Night has achieved a 400-year-old niche in the national memory, and despite the window it opens on to an earlier world of hatred and fear, its present position is due more to a reinterpretation than to a continuity of tradition. It may now be a simple delight in shared bonfires and fireworks that gives the Fifth of November so secure a place in our calendar that it will never be forgot.